Introduction

The aims of *Cambridge English for Nursing* are to improve your communication skills at work and your English language knowledge in key areas of nursing. To give you practice in current healthcare situations, each of the ten units contains:

- discussion of the nursing topic
- listening activities reflecting everyday nursing scenarios
- a focus on communication, for example giving advice sensitively
- a medical focus, for example describing how the heart works
- charting and documentation – medical forms and how to use them
- abbreviations and acronyms used in healthcare
- an online glossary with a pronunciation guide

On the audio you hear people in the kind of healthcare situations that you encounter as a nurse, for example admitting a patient, explaining medical procedures, discussing lifestyle changes, handing over patients, taking part in training sessions, preparing a pre-op patient, and dealing with young patients in pain. In addition, online activities focusing on advances in technology will help you keep up-to-date with the latest medical equipment.

How to use *Cambridge English for Nursing* for self-study

If you are working on your own, you can do the units in any order you like. Choose the topic that you want to look at and work through the unit doing the exercises and checking your answers in the answer key. Note down any mistakes you make, and go back and listen or read again to see what the problem was. It's a good idea to listen to the audio more than once and to read the audioscript afterwards to check that you've understood. For the speaking activities, *think* about what you would say in the situation. You could also try talking about the discussion points with your colleagues; the topics are all relevant for people who work in healthcare. Audioscripts and a comprehensive answer key with solutions to the activities as well as suggested answers for the discussion tasks are at the back of the book. In addition, you can find extra material and further activities for practice online at www.cambridge.org/elt/englishfornursing.

We hope you enjoy using the course. If you have any comments on *Cambridge English for Nursing*, we'd love to hear them. You can email us at englishfornursing@cambridge.org.

Virginia   *Patricia*

Virginia Allum (BA, MA, Cert TESOL, Certificate in Nursing) lives and works in Australia and has extensive experience as a Registered Nurse working in hospitals in Sydney and on the Gold Coast. She also has palliative care experience gained while working as Director of a home nursing service in Sydney. She has taught English for nursing at a vocational training institute in Queensland and also works as a Lecturer and Nurse Facilitator in the diploma of nursing at the Gold Coast Institute of TAFE (Technical and Further Education) in Queensland.

Patricia McGarr (B Ed, Dip TESOL, MA TESOL, MBA) lives in Australia and works at Griffith University. She has wide-ranging international teaching experience, having managed a network of language institutes in Asia, project managed specialised English courses in Kuwait and Oman, and been instrumental in setting up industry-specific language projects in Vietnam and China. She managed the Insearch Language Centre, University of Technology, Sydney – one of the largest English language institutes in Australia – and set up several offshore programs that they delivered in Asia.

	Skills	Medical focus	Charting and documentation
UNIT 1 Patient admissions page 6	Taking a patient history Using active listening strategies Explaining how the heart works Putting a patient at ease Giving a nursing handover Charting blood pressure and pulse	The heart Explaining how the heart works	Patient Admission Form Patient Record Observation Chart
UNIT 2 Respiratory problems page 14	Educating patients about asthma management Giving instructions effectively Using a nebuliser Talking to a child about asthma Putting a young patient at ease Describing respiration Charting respiratory rates	The respiratory system	Respiratory rates Patient record Observation chart
UNIT 3 Wound care page 22	Discussing wound management Asking for advice Describing wounds Taking part in Continuous Professional Development Using a Wound Assessment Chart	Wound bed preparation	Wound Assessment Chart
UNIT 4 Diabetes care page 30	Discussing diabetes management Making empathetic responses Giving advice sensitively Using a Diabetic Chart	The pancreas Explaining hypoglycaemia and diabetes	Diabetic Chart
UNIT 5 Medical specimens page 38	Explaining pathology tests Asking for clarification Checking understanding Telephone skills: contacting other staff Softening a request Reading a Pathology Report	The kidneys Explaining renal failure Explaining urinary catheters	Pathology Report
UNIT 6 Medications page 46	Administering medication Doing a medication check Working as part of a team Checking medication orders for accuracy Explaining drug interactions Checking the 'five rights' of medication administration Reading a Prescription Chart	The metabolism of medication	Prescription Chart

	Skills	Medical focus	Charting and documentation
UNIT 7 Intravenous infusions page 54	Reviewing IV infusions Passing on instructions to colleagues Assessing IV cannulas Telephone skills: taking a message about patient care Checking IV orders Charting fluid intake and output	IV cannulas	IV Prescription Chart Fluid Balance Chart
UNIT 8 Pre-operative patient assessment page 62	Doing pre-operative checks Giving pre-operative patient education Preparing a patient for surgery Allaying anxiety in a patient Using Pre-operative Checklists	Blood circulation	Pre-operative Checklist
UNIT 9 Post-operative patient assessment page 70	Giving a post-operative handover Checking a post-operative patient on the ward Explaining post-operative pain management Dealing with aggressive behaviour Using pain assessment tools	Pain receptors	Universal Pain Assessment Tool
UNIT 10 Discharge planning page 78	Attending the ward team meeting Telephone skills: referring a patient Explaining the effects of a stroke Using patient discharge planning forms	Cerebrovascular accidents	Telephone Referral Form Katz ADL Index Discharge Plan

Role plays and additional material   page 86
Audioscript   page 94
Answer key   page 110
Acknowledgements   page 120

UNIT 1 Patient admissions

- Taking a patient history
- Using active listening strategies
- Explaining how the heart works
- Putting a patient at ease
- Giving a nursing handover
- Charting blood pressure and pulse

Taking a patient history

1 **a** **In pairs, look at the picture and discuss the following questions.**

1 What do you think the nurse is doing?
2 What information might you need to collect in this situation?
3 Why might this information be important?
4 What strategies have you found useful when greeting a patient for the first time?

b ▶1.1 **Shona, the Ward Nurse, is admitting Mrs Chad. Listen to the conversation and answer the following questions.**

1 Is Mrs Chad mobile?
2 Has she been waiting long?
3 Which hospital unit is she being admitted to?

c ▶1.1 **Listen again and put the following sentences in the correct order.**

☐ How are you today?
☐ I'd like to ask you a few questions, if it's all right with you?
☐ Not too bad, thank you.
☐ Good morning, Shona.
☐ Yes, of course. That's fine.
☐1 Good morning, Mrs Chad. My name's Shona. I'll be admitting you to the ward today.

d ▶1.2 **Listen to the rest of the conversation between Shona and Mrs Chad and answer the following questions.**

1 Why is Mrs Chad in hospital?
2 What happened to her last year?
3 Does she have any allergies?
4 Does she have a relative who can be contacted during an emergency?

e ▶1.2 **Listen again and match the questions (1–7) to the answers (a–g).**

1 Can you tell me your full name, please?	a Not that I know of.
2 Can you tell me why you're here today?	b No, I'm very lucky. I never have.
3 Have you had any serious illnesses in the past?	c It's my son, Jeremy. Jeremy Chad.
4 Have you ever had any operations?	d Yes, I had a mild heart attack last year.
5 Now, are you taking any medications at the moment?	e Well, I've got high blood pressure, and I'm here for some tests.
6 Do you have any allergies to medications?	f Yes, my doctor put me on some blood pressure tablets after my heart attack.
7 Can you tell me the name of your next of kin?	g Yes, it's Doreen Mary Chad.

f **In pairs, take turns to ask and answer the questions from Exercise 1e, using the following information and your own name and next of kin.**

- I had my appendix out when I was fourteen.
- I take aspirin every day for my arthritis.
- I'm here for a chest X-ray.
- I had pneumonia two years ago.
- I'm allergic to nuts.

g **In pairs, discuss how you might change your approach for the following patients.**

1 An elderly patient who uses a walking aid
2 A young patient
3 A patient who has been waiting a long time

Communication focus: using active listening strategies

2 a **In pairs, discuss the following questions.**

1 What are active listening strategies?
2 Why do you think they are important?

b **Complete the following active listening strategies using the words and phrases in the box.**

eye contact   *mm*   nodding your head   *hm*   *I see*

1 Using expressions such as *Really?, Is that right?*, _____ and *Yes* or *No*.
2 Making 'listening noises' like _____ and _____ shows that you are interested in what the speaker is saying.
3 Leaning towards the other person and _____ also shows interest.
4 Smiling while maintaining _____ puts a patient at ease.

c ▶1.2 **Shona uses several active listening strategies whilst taking Mrs Chad's details. Listen again and find examples in the audioscript on page 94.**

d **In pairs, practise taking patient details. Student A, you are Shona; Student B, you are Mrs Chad. Remember to use active listening strategies. Swap roles and practise again.**

e   In pairs, prepare nurse–patient interviews. Student A, you are the nurse; look at the Patient Admission Form and think about the questions you will ask to complete it. Student B, you are the patient; read the patient details on page 86. Swap roles and practise again using the patient details on page 93.

THE ALEXANDRA HOSPITAL

(Patient Identification Label)

PATIENT ADMISSION FORM

Patient details	
Full name	
DOB	
Reason for admission	
Past medical history	
Past surgical history	
Medication	
Allergies	
Next of kin	

Share your knowledge

In small groups, discuss the following questions and then feed back your group's ideas to the class.

- Is the process for taking a patient history the same in your country?
- How has the introduction of privacy laws and Nursing Informatics changed the way patient information is recorded and used?
- What do you know about Electronic Patient Records (EPR)?
- Are you familiar with coding for improved patient identification?

Medical focus: the heart

Explaining how the heart works

3 **a** **In pairs, answer the following questions.**

1 What is the cardiac cycle?
2 What does the heart do during a heartbeat?
3 What symptoms does a person have if there is not enough blood flow through the heart?
4 Why might nurses in the Cardiac Unit need to explain the cardiac cycle to their patients?

b **Read the patient information leaflet. In pairs, discuss what the following parts of the heart do.**

the atria   the valves   the ventricles   the pulmonary vein
the pulmonary artery   the aorta

How does your heart work?

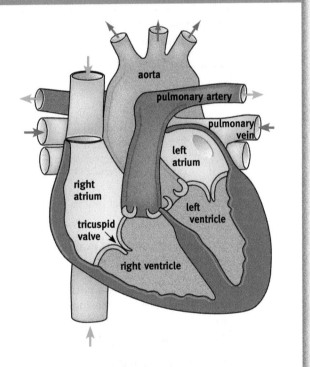

The blood enters the right atrium, one of the upper receiving chambers of the heart. Blood is pumped through the tricuspid valve into the right ventricle. The right and left ventricles are larger than the right and left atria because they are responsible for the pumping action of the heart. The right ventricle pumps de-oxygenated blood away from the heart through the T-shaped pulmonary artery. By the time blood arrives in the lungs the body has taken out most of the oxygen and made use of it for tissue function. In a healthy heart, the blood flows efficiently through the heart to the lungs, which re-oxygenate the blood and return it to the heart through the pulmonary vein. Oxygenated blood enters the heart through the left atrium and is pumped to the left ventricle. The left ventricle is encased in thicker cardiac muscle than the right side because it has to pump oxygenated blood around the entire body via the aorta, the largest artery of the body. The cardiac cycle relies on the efficiency of the four valves between the atria, the ventricles and the pulmonary blood vessels. These valves open to let in sufficient blood flow to fill each heart chamber and then shut to prevent the backflow of blood. Irregularities in blood flow because of blockages in the blood vessels can lead to heart disease.

c **In pairs, practise explaining how the heart functions. Student A, you are a nurse; Student B, you are a patient. Swap roles and practise again.**

Communication focus: putting a patient at ease

Before discussing important lifestyle changes with a patient, it is important to put the patient at ease. Sensitive topics can be broached more easily if the patient feels relaxed and comfortable.

4 a ▶1.3 **Listen to a conversation between a Nurse Educator, Susanna, and her patient, Mr Hockings. What is the topic of their discussion and why is it important?**

b **Susanna uses several informal expressions to create a friendly and relaxed relationship with the patient. Match the expressions from the dialogue (1–7) to their meanings (a–g).**

1 have a chat	a monitor
2 a bit of a shock	b I'm going to sit down
3 a bit flushed	c ruddy/red complexion
4 watch for	d take notice of
5 I'll just grab a chair	e discuss
6 fired up	f enthusiastic
7 keep an eye on	g unpleasant surprise

c **Complete the strategies for putting a patient at ease (1–4) using the words in the box. Then match them to the rationales (a–d).**

judgemental rapport positive same level

1 Sit at the _____ as the patient.	a This encourages patients in their attempts at learning new information.
2 Make _____ responses whilst nodding your head.	b This shows respect for the patient's right to make decisions about healthcare.
3 Don't make _____ comments.	c This can lighten the atmosphere and help patients relax.
4 Use humour to establish a good _____ with your patient.	d This helps patients feel that you are interested in talking to them rather than over them.

d ▶1.3 **Listen again and find examples of the strategies in Exercise 4c in the audioscript on page 94.**

e **In pairs, practise putting a patient at ease. Student A, you are Susanna; Student B, you are Mr Hockings. Remember to use active listening strategies. Swap roles and practise again.**

Share your knowledge

In small groups, discuss the following questions and then feed back your group's ideas to the class.

- What strategies do you use for putting a patient at ease?
- What difficulties have you encountered with anxious patients?
- What role does cultural sensitivity play when putting a patient at ease?

Charting and documentation: a nursing handover

Healthcare professionals write entries about patients in their care in the Patient Record. The Patient Record documents patient care and, as such, forms a permanent legal record of treatment. At the end of each nursing shift, the outgoing nurses give a verbal handover to nurses on the incoming shift. The nurses on the incoming shift are briefed on changes in patient progress and patient care. The handover is usually performed face-to-face but some institutions use recorded handovers. The information which is reported during the handover is gathered from the Patient Record, the Care Plan and any other charts which document specific patient care.

5 a **In pairs, discuss the following questions.**

1 What do you think are the features of a good handover?
2 What information does not have to be repeated in a handover? Why not?
3 What can happen if handovers do not communicate important information from one shift to another?

b ▶1.4 **Listen to Emily, a Ward Nurse, handing over a patient, Mrs Cho, and answer the following questions.**

1 What is her present medical problem?
2 What is her past medical history?

c ▶1.4 **Listen again and mark the following statements True (T) or False (F).**

1 She does not manage her ADLs at home by herself.
2 She has been quite distressed.
3 Her BP at 10 am was 200/105.
4 Her pulse was 88 at 10 am.
5 The porter has been booked for tomorrow.

d *Abbreviations are often used in both Patient Records and verbal handovers. Some are only found in written documents. It is important to check which abbreviations are approved at the hospital where you are working, as there may be some variance.*

Match the abbreviations (1–14) to their meanings (a–n).

1 BP	a activities of daily living
2 P	b four times a day
3 qds	c Senior House Officer
4 MI	d electrocardiogram
5 GTN	e sublingual, or under the tongue
6 SHO	f myocardial infarction, or heart attack
7 4°	g blood pressure
8 c/o	h complain of
9 sl	i observations
10 O_2	j four hourly, or every four hours; also 4/24
11 ECG	k patient
12 ADLs	l glyceryl trinitrate; also called nitrolingual
13 Pt	m pulse
14 obs.	n oxygen

e ▶1.4 **Listen again and complete the following extract using the abbreviations in Exercise 5d.**

Right, now Mrs Cho in bed number five. Mrs Cho was readmitted yesterday because of uncontrolled hypertension. You'll probably remember her from last week. She went home but couldn't manage her (1) _ADLs_ by herself. Her daughter had to come in every morning to give her a shower and help her during the day. She's been quite distressed about it, according to her daughter. She presented to the unit with uncontrolled hypertension, despite a change in medication. She has a past history of (2) _____ this year in June. Um, this morning she complained of chest pain. The (3) _____ was called. Her (4) _____ at the time – er, that was 10 am – was two ten over one oh five, and her pulse was one hundred. She had an (5) _____ done and was given (6) _____ sublingually. We gave her some (7) _____ via the mask and she seemed to settle. She's in for cardiac catheterisation tomorrow to assess the extent of the damage to her heart. I've booked the porter already. Strict four hourly BP and pulse and report any chest pain immediately, of course. She's had no chest pain this shift.

f **A Patient Record contains entries from every member of the patient's team. As a nurse, you must read all entries in order to plan patient care efficiently. Another patient, Mrs Smits, is handed over. Use information from the Patient Record to complete what was said.**

THE ALEXANDRA HOSPITAL

PATIENT RECORD

U/N: 732910
Surname: Smits
Given names: Livia
DOB: 10.12.31   Sex: Female

DATE & TIME	Add signature, printed name, staff category, date and time to all entries MAKE ALL NOTES CONCISE AND RELEVANT Leave no gaps between entries
18.5.2008 22.30hrs.	Mrs Smits c/o chest pain at 22.00hrs. SHO informed. O_2 administered via a mask. BP 220/100 P 120 at 22.00hrs. SHO ordered ECG, attended by nursing staff. GTN sl administered at 22.05hrs, chest pain relieved within 2 minutes. J Keene (RN) KEENE

Mrs Smits (1) ___complained of___ chest pain at (2) _____ .
The (3) _____ was informed. (4) _____ was administered via a mask. Her blood pressure was (5) _____ and her (6) _____ was (7) _____ at (8) _____ . The (9) _____ ordered an (10) _____ , which was done by nursing staff. GTN (11) _____ was given with good effect. The chest pain was relieved within a couple of minutes.

g ▶1.5 **Listen to Nick handing over Mrs Smits and check your answers. In pairs, practise the handover using only the written Patient Record.**

h **In pairs, practise giving a handover using the Patient Record. Student A, look at the record on page 86; Student B, look at the record on page 93.**

Charting blood pressure and pulse

Mrs Small has been admitted with hypertension, which has been poorly managed at home. Her doctor decides to review the medication she is taking to control her high blood pressure. For the first day after admission, her blood pressure and pulse will be observed regularly. The admitting doctor has placed her on four hourly observations of blood pressure and pulse.

6 a **In pairs, look at the chart on page 86 and discuss the following questions.**

1 Are you familiar with this type of chart?
2 What other styles of Observations Chart are you familiar with?
3 Who has access to the chart?
4 Who is responsible for completing the chart?

b ▶1.6 **Jenny, the Ward Nurse, is handing over Mrs Small to the afternoon shift. Listen to the conversation and answer the following questions.**

1 How long will Mrs Small be in hospital for?
2 Why did Dr Fielding come to see her?
3 What did Jenny do just before handover?

c ▶1.6 **Some of the information in the Obs. Chart on page 86 is incorrect. Listen again and correct any mistakes.**

d **Blood pressure readings are spoken as the first number *on* or *over* the second. For example, 90/60 is *ninety over sixty* or *ninety on sixty*. How would you say the following blood pressure readings?**

1 110/70   3 142/99
2 150/90   4 86/40

e **Look at Mrs Small's handover in the audioscript on page 94 and find phrases describing changes in her pulse or blood pressure readings. What other phrases could you use? Add them to the table.**

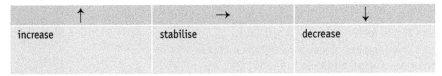

↑	→	↓
increase	stabilise	decrease

f **In pairs, practise handing over Mrs Small. Student A, you are Jenny; Student B, you are a nurse on the afternoon shift. Use the Obs. Chart on page 86, the audioscript on page 94 and the phrases in Exercise 6e. Swap roles and practise again.**

- Educating patients about asthma management
- Giving instructions effectively
- Using a nebuliser
- Talking to a child about asthma
- Putting a young patient at ease
- Describing respiration
- Charting respiratory rates

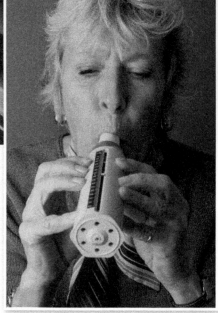

Educating patients about asthma management

1 a **In pairs, look at the picture and discuss the following questions.**

   1 What do you think this equipment is used for?
   2 Have you used this equipment before?

b ▶ **2.1 Eleanor is an Asthma Clinic Nurse. One of her roles is to educate patients in their asthma management. Listen to a conversation with a patient, Mrs Drake, and answer the following questions.**

   1 How does Mrs Drake feel?
   2 Why is Eleanor teaching her to use a peak flow meter?
   3 At what time of day should she take the reading?
   4 What three things does she have to remember?

c ▶ **2.1 Listen again and complete the following extracts.**

   1 ... a peak flow meter today. _____ if I go through it with you now?

   2 Now, _____ to use this peak flow meter at the same time every day.

   3 Another thing – _____ record your readings in this Daily Record Chart, please?

d **You are going to listen to Eleanor giving instructions on using the peak flow meter. Before you listen, put the following sentences in the correct order.**

☐ The last thing to remember is to record the highest of the three readings on your Daily Record Chart.

☐ After that, I want you to blow into the peak flow meter two more times.

☐ Next, blow as hard and as fast as you can with one breath.

☑ Right, first of all, just move the red indicator to the bottom of the numbered scale, like this.

☐ Now, stand up. Take a deep breath and try to fill your lungs as much as you can.

☐ Make a note of the final position of the marker.

e ▶ 2.2 **Listen and check your answers.**

f **Find the instructional language in the audioscript on page 95. What do you notice about the verb forms?**

Communication focus: giving instructions effectively

2 a **In pairs, discuss the following questions.**

- Do you know any techniques for giving instructions effectively?
- How can you make sure your instructions are effective?

b **Complete the strategies for giving instructions effectively (1–8) using the words and phrases in the box.**

> at the same level   demonstrate   *I'm going to teach you how to …*
> understood   repeat   ~~smiling~~   *firstly, secondly   That's right*   fingers

1 Put the listener at ease by using positive non-verbal communication such as _____ smiling _____ .

2 Sit or stand _____ as the patient.

3 Give encouragement by making remarks such as _____ , *Yes, good*, *Well done*, etc.

4 State the purpose of the communication before giving instructions, to prepare the listener for important information; for example: _____ .

5 Use a level of language which can be _____ by the listener.

6 Give instructions in steps, for example _____ , etc. You could count the steps on your _____ to make sure your patient understands you.

7 _____ instructions on the relevant piece of equipment.

8 _____ instructions and allow the listener to ask questions.

c ▶ 2.1 & 2.2 **Which of the strategies does Eleanor use with Mrs Drake? Listen again and find examples in the audioscript on page 95.**

d **In pairs, practise giving instructions on how to use the peak flow meter. Student A, you are Eleanor; Student B, you are Mrs Drake. Remember to include strategies for giving instructions effectively. Swap roles and practise again.**

Using a nebuliser

3   a   **In pairs, discuss the following questions.**

1   What is your experience of asthma management?
2   What kind of asthma treatment is available?

b   ▶2.3 **Some asthma medication is delivered to the patient using specialised equipment. Mr Dwyer's treatment plan for his asthma management is being changed. Listen to the Ward Nurse, Melanie, instructing Mr Dwyer on how to use a nebuliser for the first time and put the following steps in the correct order.**

☐ Breathe in the mist
☐ Turn on the oxygen
☐ Put on the mask
☐ Put in the medication
☐ Connect to the oxygen

c   **Match the beginnings (1–5) to the endings (a–e) to complete Melanie's instructions.**

1 First of all,	a put on the mask and tighten the elastic straps so that it fits snugly around the head.
2 Now,	b inhale the mist until it's finished.
3 Next,	c fill the chamber of the nebuliser …
4 After that,	d turn on the oxygen so the liquid medication turns into a fine mist.
5 Finally,	e attach the tubing to the oxygen outlet on the wall.

d   ▶2.3 **How does Melanie give instructions effectively? Listen again and find examples in the audioscript on page 95.**

e   **In pairs, practise giving instructions on how to use a nebuliser. Student A, you are Melanie; Student B, you are Mr Dwyer. Remember to include strategies for giving instructions effectively. Swap roles and practise again.**

Share your knowledge

In small groups, discuss the following questions and then feed back your group's ideas to the class.

● What techniques do you find most useful when giving instructions?
● What techniques are not helpful when giving instructions?
● Have you ever encountered problems when giving instructions to a patient?

Medical focus: the respiratory system

Talking to a child about asthma

Tim, a Charge Nurse on the Paediatric Respiratory Ward, is describing the normal flow of air into the lungs to Susie, an 8-year-old patient. She has been admitted after having her first serious asthma attack and needs education about managing her condition.

4 a ▶2.4 Listen to the conversation and label the parts of the respiratory system using the words in the box.

nasal cavity   alveoli   throat or pharynx   windpipe *or* trachea   oral cavity
voice box *or* larynx   pleural membrane   epiglottis   intercostal space   bronchus

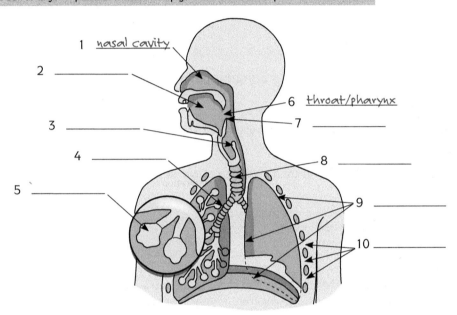

1 _nasal cavity_
2 _____
3 _____
4 _____
5 _____
6 _throat/pharynx_
7 _____
8 _____
9 _____
10 _____

b In pairs, look at the pictures of a healthy airway and an asthmatic airway and discuss the following questions.

1 What differences do you notice between the two airways?
2 How can you tell if someone is having an asthma attack?

Healthy airways   Asthmatic airways

c ▶2.5 Listen to the rest of Tim and Susie's conversation and write healthy (H) and asthmatic (A) for the following sentences.

1 a A lining of healthy tissue which is not swollen.
  b A thickened lining of tissue which is often inflamed.
2 a The contracting muscle layer makes breathing more difficult.
  b The contracting muscle layer helps conduct air into and out of the alveoli.
3 a Gas exchange occurs in the tiny air sacs called alveoli.
  b The exchange of carbon dioxide and oxygen is hindered by narrowed airways.
4 a Wheezing sounds indicate respiratory effort.
  b Respiration is quiet and easy.

d ▶2.5 **Listen again and complete the following flowchart. What do you notice about the verb forms in 1−4?**

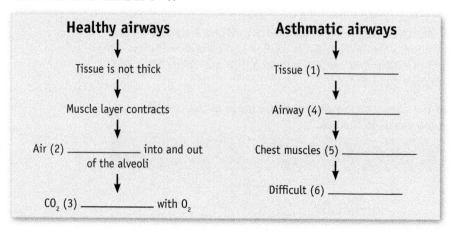

Healthy airways

↓

Tissue is not thick

↓

Muscle layer contracts

↓

Air (2) _____ into and out
of the alveoli

↓

CO_2 (3) _____ with O_2

Asthmatic airways

↓

Tissue (1) _____

↓

Airway (4) _____

↓

Chest muscles (5) _____

↓

Difficult (6) _____

Communication focus: putting a young patient at ease

5 a In pairs, discuss the following questions.

- What strategies can you use to put a young patient at ease?
- Have you used any of these strategies yourself? Were they successful?

b Complete the strategies for putting a young patient at ease (1−8) using the words in the box.

> simple ~~small talk~~ encouragement diagrams explain
> cheerful appeal level decision-making

1 Use __small talk__ , for example asking about the child's hobbies or interests.
2 Stand or sit at the same _____ as the child.
3 Use _____ , clear sentences and check for understanding.
4 Use pictures or _____ to illustrate what you are saying.
5 Involve the child in _____ , for example: *Let's call this one healthy airways − does that sound like a good idea?*
6 Give _____ .
7 Use short, simple phrases which _____ to children, for example: *the little flap.*
8 Use a _____ tone of voice.
9 _____ medical terminology in simple terms.

c ▶2.4 & 2.5 **Which of the strategies does Tim use with Susie? Listen to the whole conversation again and find examples in the audioscript on page 95.**

d In pairs, practise the dialogue. Swap roles and practise again.

e *Natalie, a 10-year-old asthmatic, has been admitted after a severe asthma attack. This is the first asthma attack she has suffered. Candy, the Nurse Educator in the Respiratory Unit, needs to explain what happens to the airways when Natalie has an asthma attack.*

In pairs, use the diagram of healthy airways and asthmatic airways on page 17 to explain what happens in an asthma attack. Student A, you are Candy; Student B, you are Natalie. Remember to use strategies for putting a young patient at ease. Swap roles and practise again.

Describing respiration

6 **a** Match the medical terms (1–7) to their meanings (a–g).

1 inspiration	a at four litres per minute
2 inspiratory rate	b the rate at which a person breathes out (expressed as breaths per minute)
3 respirations	c breaths – that is, movement of air in and out of the lungs
4 respiratory rate	d the rate at which a person breathes in (expressed as breaths per minute)
5 expiration	e breathing in
6 expiratory rate	f the rate at which a person breathes in and out (expressed as breaths per minute)
7 @ 4L/min	g breathing out

b Underline the stressed syllable in words 1–6.

c In pairs, take turns to say a word and ask your partner to define it, or give a definition and ask for the word.

d ▶ 2.6 Listen to four extracts from conversations on a ward and answer the following questions. Pay attention to the pronounciation of the words in Exercise 6a.

1   Why are Mr Frank's family going to stay with him tonight?
2   How is Judy managing her pain?
3   How was oxygen administered to Mr Walker?
4   What caused Mr Sims' tachypnoea?

e In pairs, look at Mrs Oondahi's Nursing Notes and ask and answer questions using the prompt cards. Student A, turn to page 86; Student B, turn to page 93.

DATE & TIME	Add signature, printed name, staff category, date and time to all entries MAKE ALL NOTES CONCISE AND RELEVANT Leave no gaps between entries
2.3.09 21.00hrs	NURSING Mrs Oondahi appears to be breathing comfortably at the time of the report and is quite settled. RR is 16, not laboured. O_2 @ 3L/min via nasal cannulae. Pt lying on two pillows. Pain relieved by morphine via continuous s.c infusion. Pain rated at 1/10 at 20.30hrs. Patient states she is comfortable. Family in attendance all shift. Husband and children will stay overnight with her. <div align="right">D. Simpson (RN) SIMPSON</div>

Share your knowledge

In small groups, discuss the following questions and then feed back your group's ideas to the class.

- Are family members / partners permitted to stay with a dying patient in hospital in your country?
- What are the benefits of allowing this arrangement?
- Are there any difficulties with this arrangement?
- Why is it important to be culturally sensitive in this type of situation?

Charting and documentation: respiratory rates

7 a Mr Wilmott, an 86-year-old who lives alone, has been admitted to hospital for treatment. In pairs, look at his record and discuss the following questions.

1 What is Mr Wilmott's diagnosis?
2 What is the treatment?
3 What is happening in the morning?
4 What respiratory assessment has he started doing himself?

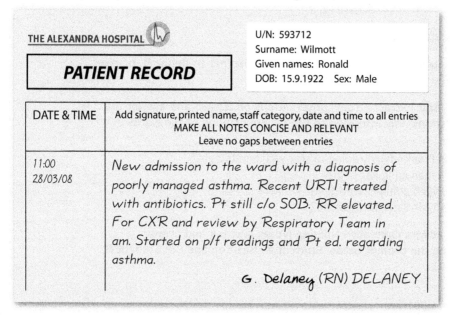

THE ALEXANDRA HOSPITAL

PATIENT RECORD

U/N: 593712
Surname: Wilmott
Given names: Ronald
DOB: 15.9.1922   Sex: Male

DATE & TIME	Add signature, printed name, staff category, date and time to all entries MAKE ALL NOTES CONCISE AND RELEVANT Leave no gaps between entries
11:00 28/03/08	New admission to the ward with a diagnosis of poorly managed asthma. Recent URTI treated with antibiotics. Pt still c/o SOB. RR elevated. For CXR and review by Respiratory Team in am. Started on p/f readings and Pt ed. regarding asthma. G. Delaney (RN) DELANEY

b Match the abbreviations from the Patient Record (1–6) to their meanings (a–f).

1 URTI	a respiratory rate
2 SOB	b peak flow; the most air which is expired
3 RR	c chest X-ray
4 CXR	d patient education
5 p/f	e upper respiratory tract infection
6 Pt ed.	f shortness of breath; difficulty breathing (dyspnoea)

c In pairs, take turns to ask for the meaning of an abbreviation.

d ▶2.7 Mrs Castle is a 56-year-old with a past history of respiratory problems relating to chronic asthma. Listen to a conversation between two Ward Nurses, Mandy and Rosa, and answer the following questions.

1 How often is Mrs Castle having her respiratory rate checked?
2 How much oxygen was she having when she returned from her operation?
3 Why was she given oxygen?
4 How long will Mandy be away?

e ▶2.7 Some of the information on Mrs Castle's Obs. Chart on page 87 is incorrect. Listen again and correct any mistakes.

f Match the medical terms (1–5) to their meanings (a–e).

1 apnoea	a the patient has laboured breathing or difficulty breathing
2 bradypnoea	b the patient is not breathing at all
3 eupnoea	c the respiratory rate is rapid; it has increased to between 20 and 30 breaths per minute
4 tachypnoea	d the patient's breathing is slow rate; the respiratory rate is less than 12 breaths per minute
5 dyspnoea	e the patient is breathing a normal respiratory rate – between 12 and 20 breaths per minute

g Underline the stressed syllable in words 1–5.

h In pairs, answer the following questions.

1 The word element *-pnoea* (US *-pnea*) means *breathing*. Is the *p* a silent letter in all words which are formed using this word element?
2 If not, which word(s) in Exercise 6f do not have a silent *p*?

i Read the entry in Mrs Castle's Patient Record made by Dr Smith, the Senior House Officer, and answer the following questions.

1 What do the abbreviations AE and FBC stand for?
2 Does Mrs Castle have a high temperature?
3 Are her respirations fast or slow?
4 When will she have the blood test done?
5 Was she taking aspirin before?

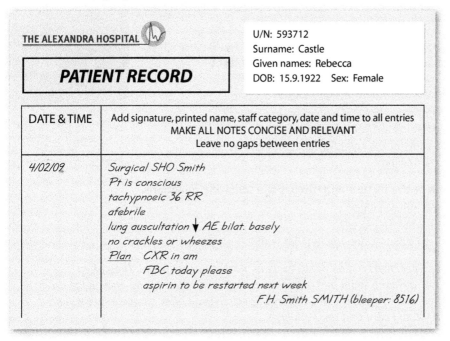

THE ALEXANDRA HOSPITAL

PATIENT RECORD

U/N: 593712
Surname: Castle
Given names: Rebecca
DOB: 15.9.1922   Sex: Female

DATE & TIME	Add signature, printed name, staff category, date and time to all entries MAKE ALL NOTES CONCISE AND RELEVANT Leave no gaps between entries

4/02/09	Surgical SHO Smith
	Pt is conscious
	tachypnoeic 36 RR
	afebrile
	lung auscultation ↓ AE bilat. basely
	no crackles or wheezes
	Plan CXR in am
	         FBC today please
	         aspirin to be restarted next week
	                    F.H. Smith SMITH (bleeper: 8516)

j In pairs, take turns to ask and answer more questions about Mrs Castle's Patient Record. Student A, you are handing over Mrs Castle to Student B. Swap roles and practise again.

- Discussing wound management
- Asking for advice
- Describing wounds
- Taking part in Continuous Professional Development
- Using a Wound Assessment Chart

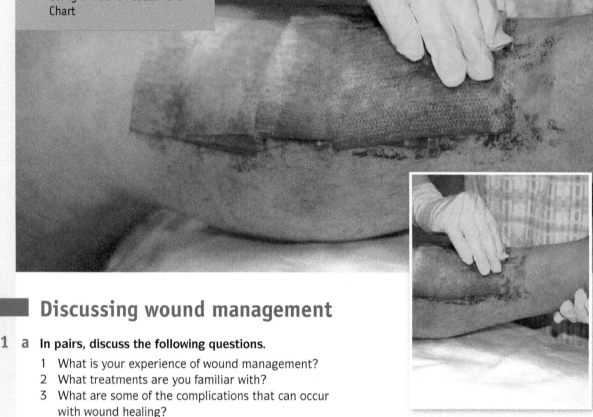

Discussing wound management

1 a In pairs, discuss the following questions.

1 What is your experience of wound management?
2 What treatments are you familiar with?
3 What are some of the complications that can occur with wound healing?

b In pairs, look at the picture and discuss the following questions.

1 What is the nurse doing?
2 Why is she wearing gloves?
3 What wound closures are you familiar with?

c *Clinical Nurse Specialists act as consultants in most large hospitals. They often work as part of a Health Team and assist ward staff when specialised knowledge is required. Some of the areas a Clinical Nurse Specialist will offer advice in are wound management, stoma care and renal dialysis.*

▶3.1 **Listen to a conversation between Sophie, a Clinical Nurse Specialist, and Ali, a Ward Nurse, and answer the following questions.**

1 Why has Ali asked Sophie to come to the ward?
2 What kind of wound does Mr Jones have?
3 How long has he been in hospital this admission?

d **Put the following sentences in the correct order.**

- ☐ He had a Doppler test done last week.
- ☐ We sent a wound swab off, and we just got the results yesterday.
- ☐ Mr Jones is a 68-year-old smoker with a long history of PVD.
- ☐ He's started on some IV antibiotics.
- ☐ Two weeks ago he was admitted to this ward to have an assessment of his circulation and to monitor his wound management.
- ☐ He developed a venous ulcer on his right ankle after he tripped on some stairs …
- ☐ His local doctor had a look at it and asked the District Nurses to come and dress the wound at home.

e ▶3.1 **Listen again and check your answers.**

f **Match the medical terms and abbreviations (1–7) to their meanings (a–g).**

1 CNS	a microbes
2 PVD	b ultrasound device which measures blood flow through arteries and veins
3 Doppler	c have episodes of pyrexia
4 bugs	d antibiotics which are given through a vein
5 spike a temperature	e Vacuum Assisted Closure; also pronounced *vac*
6 IV ABs	f Clinical Nurse Specialist
7 VAC	g Peripheral Vascular Disease

g ▶3.2 **Listen to a conversation between Sophie, Ali and Mr Jones and answer the following questions.**

1 Why is Mr Jones's ulcer being reassessed?
2 What type of dressing are they going to use?
3 Why has this type of dressing been suggested?

Communication focus: asking for advice

2 a **Match the beginnings (1–5) to the endings (a–e) to complete the questions.**

1 Would you mind	a that we change to?
2 What would you recommend	b use?
3 What do you think	c giving me some advice on his wound care management?
4 What do you suggest we	d to try that instead of the dressing they're using now?
5 Do you think it's a good idea	e I should do with this ulcer?

b **Match the sentences in Exercise 2a to the most likely responses.**

1 _____
Well, I think the first thing to do is to reassess the wound.

2 _____
I'd like to use a VAC dressing on this wound.

3 _____
No, not at all. That's what I'm here for.

4 _____
Let me have a look at the wound and we'll see what the best option is.

5 _____
Yes. I think it'll help the wound heal faster.

c   In pairs, practise asking for and giving advice on the treatment of Mr Jones'
    ulcer. Student A, you are the Ward Nurse; Student B, you are the wound
    management Clinical Nurse Specialist. Swap roles and practise again.

Share your knowledge

**In small groups, discuss the following questions and then feed back
your group's ideas to the class.**

- Do you have wound management Clinical Nurse Specialists in your
  country?
- If not, how do you get advice on managing chronic wounds?

Medical focus: wound bed preparation

Describing wounds

*The progress of wound treatment is monitored and recorded in a Clinical
Pathway or Integrated Care Pathway (ICP) document. A specialised wound chart
describes the dimensions of the wound, the type of discharge from the wound
and the presence or absence of infection.*

3   a   **In pairs, look at the pictures of wounds (a–d) and discuss the following
        questions.**

    1   How would you describe the wounds?
    2   How would you manage them?

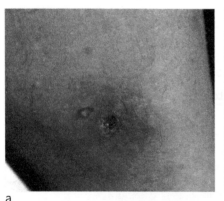

a

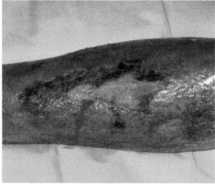

b

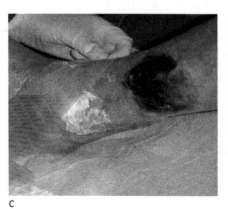

c

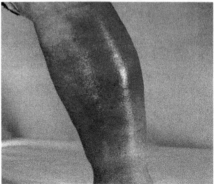

d

b **Match the medical terms (1–8) to their meanings (a–h).**

1 necrosis		a	thick, dry, black necrotic tissue
2 eschar		b	drying out
3 desiccation		c	inflammation of the tissue under the skin, often caused by infection
4 inflammation		d	a small piece of material which is used to take samples of body fluids
5 swab		e	dead tissue which separates from healthy tissue after infection
6 slough		f	the removal of dead tissue
7 debridement		g	swelling caused by infection
8 cellulitis		h	death of cells and living tissue

c **Underline the stressed syllable in words 1–8.**

d **In pairs, take turns to say a word and ask your partner to define it.**

e **Complete the following sentences using the words in the box and then match the sentences to the photos in Exercise 3a.**

> cellulitis   slough   eschar   inflammation   swab   necrosis   desiccation   debridement

1 Mrs Ximenes has an area of ___necrosis___ , or dead tissue, on her left lower leg. There are blackened areas, or _____ , on the upper wound. These areas will be surgically debrided tomorrow.
   photo _____

2 Mr Edwards has _____ in the lower leg. The wound is showing signs of drying out, or _____ – there is quite a lot of skin flaking off his leg.
   photo _____

3 The skin surrounding Mrs Heath's leg wound is red and warm to the touch. The _____ is a sign of infection and was confirmed by a wound _____ sent to the Pathology lab three days ago.
   photo _____

4 The yellowish _____ , or dead fibrous tissue, on the inner part of Birad's wound will have to be softened before _____ , or removal of the tissue, is possible.
   photo _____

f **In pairs, take turns to describe the wounds in Exercise 3a.**

Share your knowledge

1 Diabetic ulcers, also called neurotrophic ulcers, are usually found on the balls of the feet at the points of maximum pressure. What sorts of difficulties would the location of these ulcers cause?

2 What advice would you give diabetics about footwear?

3 What may occur as the consequence of diabetic ulcers?

Taking part in Continuous Professional Development (CPD)

Continuous Professional Development is a major workplace focus for nurses and is a requirement for continuing registration in some countries. It ensures that nurses keep up-to-date with current trends in clinical practice, such as Evidence-Based Practice (EBP) and risk management clinical governance.

4 **a In pairs, discuss the following questions.**

- What is your experience of Continuous Professional Development?
- Are you familiar with sharing your knowledge through feedback sessions on the ward? If not, how do you share your knowledge with your colleagues?

b ▶3.3 You are attending a CPD training session given by a wound management Clinical Nurse Specialist, Mr John Simpkins, on wound bed preparation. Listen and tick the medical terms you hear (1–8).

1 ☑ well-vascularised	a the transplantation of skin from another part of the body to a wound which cannot heal on its own
2 ☐ viable	b excessive softness caused by too much moisture
3 ☐ necrotic tissue	c good blood circulation is achieved, and the tissues are supplied with oxygen and other nutrients
4 ☐ high bacterial load	d long-term or ongoing
5 ☐ exudate	e a high level of infection carried by the tissues
6 ☐ maceration	f ooze or discharge from a wound
7 ☐ chronic	g able to grow or survive
8 ☐ skin graft	h dead tissue

c Match the medical terms above (1–8) to their meanings (a–h).

d In pairs, take turns to say a word and ask your partner to define it.

e ▶3.3 Listen again and complete the following handout using the words in the box.

> necrosis   exudate   dryness   load   balance   inflammation   ~~stable~~   base

---

SESSION HANDOUT

The aim of wound bed preparation is to prepare a (1) _____stable_____ wound environment which results in wound healing.

This is achieved by:
a)   restoring a well-vascularised wound bed, or (2) _____
b)   decreasing the high bacterial load by controlling (3) _____ or infection
c)   creating moisture (4) _____ in the wound environment

The barriers to wound healing include:
a)   the presence of (5) _____ – in other words, dead tissue
b)   high bacterial (6) _____ , or a high level of infection carried by the tissues
c)   imbalance of moisture levels: wounds with excessive (7) _____ – that is, wounds which are too moist – and wounds which have excessive (8) _____ , or desiccation, will not heal properly

---

f ▶ 3.4 **Listen to the second part of the training session and complete the rest of the handout using the words in the box.**

dressings graft debridement infection ~~viable~~ imbalance excessive reassess antibiotic
desiccation reduced optimal fluid chronic well-vascularised advanced surgical

What is TIME? TIME is an acronym for a framework which helps to identify barriers to healing in the wound bed and identifies expected outcomes of treatment.				
	T	**I**	**M**	**E**
Description of the wound	Tissue is not (1) ___viable___. The tissues of the wound bed do not have sufficient blood supply to survive.	Inflammation or (5) _____ is present. The high bacterial load prevents healing.	Moisture (8) _____. (9) _____ exudate causes maceration, or softening, of the wound edges. (10) _____, or excessive dryness, slows healing.	Edge of the wound does not heal. The wound becomes a (14) _____ wound.
Clinical action	(2) _____ of necrotic tissue. Often a (3) _____ procedure.	Remove the infection and reduce the high bacterial load. Antimicrobial dressings as well as (6) _____ medication are used.	Hydrating (11) _____, which add moisture for dry wounds. Negative pressure dressings, e.g. VAC dressings, which remove excess (12) _____ in macerated wounds.	(15) _____ the wound. Consider different management, e.g. skin (16) _____ to replace the damaged skin.
Expected outcome	Wound bed is (4) _____ and has a good blood supply.	(7) _____ inflammation around the wound.	The wound has an (13) _____ moisture balance.	The edge of the wound has (17) _____ or healed.

Share your knowledge

In small groups, discuss the following questions and then feed back your group's ideas to the class.

- Do you follow the same process for wound bed preparation?
- What are the advantages of following the wound bed preparation protocol?
- Have you ever had any experience with skin grafts? If so, what type?

Charting and documentation: Wound Assessment Chart

5 a **In pairs, discuss the following questions.**

1 What is your experience of treating animal bites or wounds?
2 What complications can arise?
3 How can these complications be avoided?

b ▶3.5 **Gary Stephens has presented to Accident and Emergency with a severe dog bite wound. Listen to a conversation between Gary and two A&E nurses, Krisztina and Judy, and answer the following questions.**

1 What kind of dog bites are a serious infection risk?
2 How will Gary's wound be treated?

c ▶3.5 **The conversation contains several examples of asking for and giving advice. Listen again and match the requests (1–4) to the advice (a–d).**

1 Krisztina, what do you suggest I clean the wound with?	a Sure ... I'd like you to keep the dressing clean and dry and come to Outpatients to have the dressing changed daily.
2 Can you give me some advice on looking after this at home?	b Yes, that'd be a good idea.
3 What should I do about the antibiotics?	c It's best to flush it with lots of Normal Saline before you do the dressing.
4 Should I get a medical certificate?	d You'll be prescribed some antibiotics by the doctor a bit later. You'll get a script which you can take to the hospital pharmacy to be filled.

d ▶3.6 **Jennifer, the Ward Nurse, is handing over Gary Stephens to the afternoon shift. Listen to the handover and put the following stages described in the handover in the correct order.**

☐ Gary was started on IV antibiotics to clear up the infection in the wound.
☐ He is in for a review by the Vascular Team on Monday.
☐ The wound was surgically debrided this morning.
☐1 Gary Stephens sustained some deep puncture wounds in his left calf after a dog bite.
☐ He was treated in A&E and discharged home.
☐ Gary returned to the ward with an antimicrobial dressing which will be re-dressed tomorrow.
☐ The wound was reassessed yesterday.
☐ The wound became infected and he has returned to hospital.

e **Match the medical terms (1–12) to their meanings (a–l).**

1 granulated	a with yellowish fluid or blood serum
2 sloughy	b adding moisture to something
3 macerated	c a dressing which does not stick to the wound
4 inflamed	d contains dead tissue which falls off a wound during an infection
5 serous	e the dressing is sealed and cannot be lifted off for viewing
6 haemoserous	f full of pus, a yellow or green discharge found in an infected wound
7 purulent	g containing connective tissue found in healing wounds
8 odour	h something which treats infective microorganisms
9 non-adhesive dressing (NAD)	i softened because of excess moisture
10 antimicrobial	j yellowish fluid tinged with red blood cells
11 hydrating	k red and swollen because of infection
12 intact wound	l smell (usually unpleasant)

f   Underline the stressed syllable in words 1–12.

g   In pairs, take turns to say a word and ask your partner to define it.

h   Look at the Wound Assessment Chart. In small groups, discuss your experience if you have used a chart like this before.

THE ALEXANDRA HOSPITAL

WOUND ASSESSMENT CHART

Ward _____ 12B _____

Consultant _____ H. Perowne _____

U/N: 376442
Surname: Stephens
Given names: Gary
DOB: 5.01.1974   Sex: Male

WOUND ASSESSMENT FORM				
Date	8/2/2008			
Name	Gary Stephens			
Wound site	L calf			
Wound description	granulated	sloughy	necrotic	infected
Frequency of dressing	bd	tds	daily	3rd daily
Antibiotics	no	yes	oral	IV
Surrounding skin	healthy	dry	macerated	inflamed
Exudate	nil	small amt	moderate	heavy
Exudate – type	N/A	serous	haemoserous	purulent
Odour present	yes		no	
Debridement	nil	surgical	mechanical (wet to dry dressings)	chemical
Dressing products	non-adhesive dressing (NAD) antimicrobial hydrating			
Wound closure	sutures clips open wound			
Comments	For review by Vascular Team on Mon Wound intact – next dressing in two days			

i   Find abbreviations in the Wound Assessment Chart with the following meanings.
   1   not applicable
   2   three times a day
   3   twice a day
   4   left
   5   intravenous
   6   amount

j   ▶ 3.6 Listen again to the handover of Gary Stephens and underline the information you hear about his wound in the Wound Assessment Chart.

k   In pairs, practise handing over Gary Stephens. Student A, you are Jennifer; Student B, you are a nurse on the next shift. You can change the description of the wound using vocabulary from Exercise 5e. Swap roles and practise again.

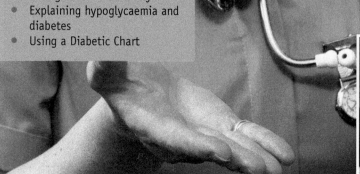

UNIT 4 Diabetes care

- Discussing diabetes management
- Making empathetic responses
- Giving advice sensitively
- Explaining hypoglycaemia and diabetes
- Using a Diabetic Chart

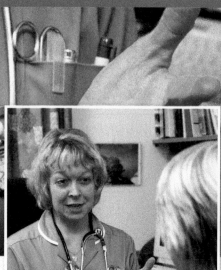

Discussing diabetes management

1 a **In pairs, discuss the following questions.**

1 Is diabetes a serious problem in your country?
2 What are your experiences of dealing with patients with diabetes?
3 What do you think is happening in the picture?

b ▶4.1 **Listen to a conversation between Mrs Kim, a diabetic patient, and Susan, the Diabetic Clinic Nurse, and answer the following questions.**

1 What is the main purpose of Mrs Kim's visit?
2 Who looked after her before she started at the Diabetic Clinic?
3 Why was she in hospital last week?

c ▶4.1 **Listen again and mark the following statements True (T) or False (F).**

1 The Diabetic Clinic referred Mrs Kim to the hospital.
2 She no longer requires a Personal Care Plan.
3 The Primary Care Team is a network of the Diabetic Clinic, the local doctor and the patient.

d **Look at the rest of the conversation and complete Susan's questions.**

Susan: (1) _____ do you see your local doctor?

Mrs Kim: I see her at least once a month for a checkup.

Susan: (2) _____ do you check your BSLs, your blood sugar levels?

Mrs Kim: At the moment I check before meals and just before I go to bed.

Susan: Do you find it easy to use the glucometer?

Mrs Kim: It's easy now. I can manage it quite well. My GP showed me how to use it.

Susan: That's good. I know what you mean; they are a bit difficult at first.
(3) _____ do you have a urine test to check your kidney function?

Mrs Kim:	Once a year. I have it all done at once. I have the urine test, the eye exam to check for retinal damage and my feet examined for nerve or circulation problems. I did have some eye problems a while back and my feet have been bothering me lately.
Susan:	Oh, that's a pity. Unfortunately, diabetes management isn't just about sugar control. There are quite a few things which need to be checked as well. (4) _____ have any hypos? I mean, any hypoglycaemic attacks?
Mrs Kim:	Only occasionally. It usually happens if I skip too many meals.
Susan:	Mm, it is very important to eat on time. (5) _____ go to the podiatrist to have your nails cut?
Mrs Kim:	Yes, I do now. I used to try to do it myself but I got a nasty infection once.
Susan:	Oh, that's not so good. I'm glad you go to the podiatrist now.

e **In pairs, use these prompts to ask and answer questions between a nurse and a diabetic patient. Swap roles and practise again.**

- use a glucometer
- eye examination
- check weight
- exercise
- have your feet checked
- check cholesterol level
- have insulin injections
- skip meals

Communication focus: making empathetic responses

Making empathetic responses encourages open communication and indicates emotional support by the listener. A rising then falling intonation is often used with expressions indicating understanding and support; for example: Oh dear / Oh, that's not good / I'm sorry to hear that / Mm.

2 a **Look at the conversations between Mrs Kim and Susan in Exercise 1d and the audioscript on page 97 and find examples of Susan's empathetic reponses.**

b **In pairs, practise giving empathetic responses. Use the questions from Exercise 1d and the prompts from Exercise 1e. Swap roles and practise again.**

Communication focus: giving advice sensitively

Mr Harry Williams, a 68-year-old insulin-dependent diabetic, has lived on his own since his wife died five years ago. He is overweight and rarely does any exercise. He used to like walking along the beach with his wife but hardly ever goes to the beach now. He has become very careless about eating regular meals and, as a result, his blood sugar levels are not stable. He used to have one or two glasses of beer every night but recently his intake has increased. He also smokes about two packets of cigarettes a week. Mr Williams has come to the Diabetic Clinic to discuss lifestyle and nutritional changes.

3 a **In pairs, discuss the following questions.**

1 What simple but significant changes should Mr Williams make to his lifestyle?
2 What is your experience of persuading elderly patients to change their lifestyle?
3 What strategies have you found to be the most successful?

b ▶4.2 **Listen to a conversation between Mr Williams and Marta, the Ward Nurse, and see how many of your ideas about lifestyle changes are mentioned.**

c ▶4.2 **Listen again and complete the following sentences.**

1 You ____'ll____ ____have____ ____to____ make some major lifestyle changes if you're going to avoid nasty complications of diabetes.
2 You _____ _____ reduce your intake of saturated fats.
3 _____ _____ make sure you include carbohydrates in each meal.
4 You really _____ keep a close eye on your weight.
5 It would be a _____ _____ to get back to walking along the beach again.
6 You _____ keep a close eye on your alcohol intake because it can affect your insulin dose.
7 ... it is _____ _____ stop smoking if you want to avoid circulation problems.
8 You _____ _____ _____ speak to your doctor about some nicotine patches.

d **In pairs, discuss the following questions.**
- What strategies have you used to give advice sensitively?
- What successes have you had?
- Why might patients reject your advice?

e **Marta uses several strategies for giving advice sensitively. Match the strategies (1–7) to the expressions from the dialogue (a–g).**

1 Justify advice	a Could you try to include ...
2 Involve the patient in decisions	b ... it can be a problem for diabetics ...
3 Acknowledge that something may be difficult to achieve	c You must keep a close eye on ...
4 Be firm but non-aggressive	d I know it must be difficult for you ...
5 Use impersonal statements, which are less threatening	e ... it is important to stop smoking if you want to avoid ...
6 Personalise the information	f It would be a good idea to get back to walking along the beach again.
7 Put the responsibility of the outcome on the patient if the advice is not taken, in a firm but supportive tone	g You'll have to ... if you're going to avoid ...

f **In pairs, practise asking for and giving advice on the following topics. Student A, you are a nurse; Student B, you are a diabetic patient. Remember to use the strategies for giving advice sensitively. Swap roles and practise again.**
- weight control
- smoking
- alcohol
- coffee
- stress
- cholesterol level

g **In pairs, prepare nurse–patient interviews. Student A, you are the patient; read your profile on page 87 and be ready to answer the nurse's questions. Student B, you are the nurse; read the patient profile on page 87. Ask questions about lifestyle and give advice on managing diabetes. Swap roles, using the patient profile on page 93.**

Medical focus: the pancreas

4 **a** **Read the information leaflet and answer the following questions.**

1 What is the exocrine function of the pancreas?
2 What is the endocrine role of the pancreas in diabetes management?
3 What does insulin do to blood sugar levels?
4 What hormone has the opposite function to insulin?

The pancreas is a small L-shaped organ which sits against the duodenum behind the stomach. It is quite small, at around 15 cm long. The pancreatic duct runs along the middle of the pancreas and empties into the duodenum. It supplies pancreatic enzymes, also called pancreatic juices, which aid in the digestion process. This is described as the exocrine function of the pancreas, *exo* meaning 'out of'. Pancreatic juices flow out of the pancreas through the pancreatic duct. The pancreatic duct is joined by the common bile duct before emptying into the duodenum. The pancreas also has an endocrine function, *endo* meaning 'within'. This is the release of hormone within the bloodstream. There are four main types of hormone produced in the hormone-producing cells of the pancreas – the islets of Langerhans (islet cells). One of the four cell types – beta cells – produce insulin. The function of insulin is to lower the blood sugar level. Beta cells make up almost eighty percent of all islet cells. Alpha cells make up almost twenty percent, and these release glucagon, which raises the level of glucose in the blood. This is the opposite function to insulin. The level of glucose in the blood is called either blood sugar level (BSL) or blood glucose level (BGL). Insulin stimulates cells in the body to use or store the glucose produced from the metabolism of carbohydrates in food. Glucose is used in the body as an energy source.

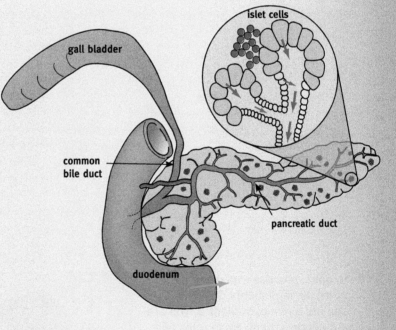

b **In pairs, practise explaining the role of the pancreas to a patient who has recently been diagnosed with diabetes. Student A, you are the nurse; Student B, you are the patient. Swap roles and practise again.**

Explaining hypoglycaemia and diabetes

5 **a** Match the medical terms (1–10) to their meanings (a–j).

1 pancreas	a the condition where the blood is more acidic than the surrounding tissues
2 diabetes	b oral medication used to lower blood sugar levels
3 diabetic	c the organ which produces insulin, which regulates blood sugar
4 hypoglycaemia	d a person who suffers from diabetes
5 hypoglycaemic agent	e disease characterised by high levels of sugar in the blood
6 glycosuria	f the by-product produced when fats metabolise
7 ketones	g hormone produced in the beta cells of the pancreas
8 diabetic ketoacidosis (DKA)	h presence of glucose in the urine
9 insulin	i amount of glucose in the blood
10 blood sugar level (BSL)	j a low level of sugar in the blood

b Underline the stressed syllable in words 1–10.

c ▶4.3 Complete the next part of the information leaflet using the words in the box. Then listen to a conversation between Nadia, a Diabetes Specialist, and Beth, a recently diagnosed diabetic, and check your answers.

> pumps   oral   injections   normalise   fuel   fat   regulates   inhalers
> 90%   children   beta   liver   glucose   ~~insulin~~

The normal pancreas produces a hormone called (1) _insulin_ in the beta cells. Insulin (2) _____ blood sugar levels (BSL) by moving (3) _____ from the blood into the muscle, (4) _____ and (5) _____ cells. This means that glucose can be used as (6) _____ for the body.

The diabetic pancreas may not produce any insulin at all in the (7) _____ cells, or produce too little insulin to (8) _____ blood sugar levels. If no insulin is produced, this is called Type 1 diabetes and is often the cause of diabetes in (9) _____ . Daily or twice-daily (10) _____ of insulin are needed by people with Type 1 diabetes. When the pancreas produces too little insulin, this is called Type 2 diabetes and makes up about (11) _____ of all cases of diabetes. This type of diabetes may be treated with an (12) _____ hypoglycaemic medication and sometimes also with insulin injections. Two new devices, insulin (13) _____ and insulin (14) _____ , offer great improvements in lifestyle for all diabetics.

d In pairs, practise explaining the role of insulin in diabetes. Student A, you are a nurse; Student B, you are a diabetic patient. Swap roles and practise again.

e *Recent advancements in diabetes research have provided diabetic patients with a number of options to assist with the self-management of their diabetes.*

▶ 4.4 **Listen to the rest of Beth and Nadia's conversation and match the options (1–3) to the pictures (a–c).**

Option 1 _____   Option 2 _____   Option 3 _____

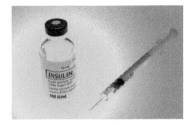      

a   b   c

f ▶ 4.4 **Listen again and complete the last part of the information leaflet.**

Option 1
- Worn all the time, delivers a
  (1) __steady__ __flow__ of
  insulin throughout the day.
- Rapid or short-acting insulin is
  delivered through a (2) _____
  placed under the skin.
- Give an extra, or (3) _____ ,
  dose to cover times when more
  carbohydrate is eaten during a meal or
  snack.
- Patient has fewer (4) _____
  _____ in blood glucose levels.
- Most expensive option.

Option 2
- Insulin is drawn up from a
  (5) _____ into a
  (6) _____ syringe.
- (7) _____ doses can be drawn
  up if needed.

- One or two types of insulin can be
  (8) _____ in the syringe.
- Markings on the side of the syringe
  can be difficult to see, which
  makes drawing up (9) _____
  _____ more difficult.
- Cheapest option but least
  (10) _____ .

Option 3
- Insulin (11) _____ fits into the
  device and can be changed.
- (12) _____-_____ devices
  are disposable and easier for diabetics
  who have arthritis or are visually
  impaired.
- Easier to use and more
  (13) _____ than syringes; can
  even fit into your pocket!
- Needle is inserted on the
  (14) _____ of the device and
  changed with each injection.

g In pairs, discuss the advantages and disadvantages of each option. Which
one would you recommend for Beth? Which one would you choose if you were
Beth?

Charting and documentation: Diabetic Chart

6 a *Mrs Alice Wilson, an insulin-dependent diabetic, has been admitted to her local hospital after a series of hypoglycaemic attacks. Mrs Wilson's blood sugar levels are being monitored closely as well as the glucose and ketone levels in her urine.*

Look at the Diabetic Chart. In pairs, answer the following questions.

1 What information is recorded on a Diabetic Chart regarding a patient's diabetes?
2 How often does Mrs Wilson have her blood sugar level taken?
3 What else does the nurse test for glucose apart from Mrs Wilson's blood?
4 What action is taken if she has a hypo?
5 What does the nurse do after she has a hypo to monitor the situation?

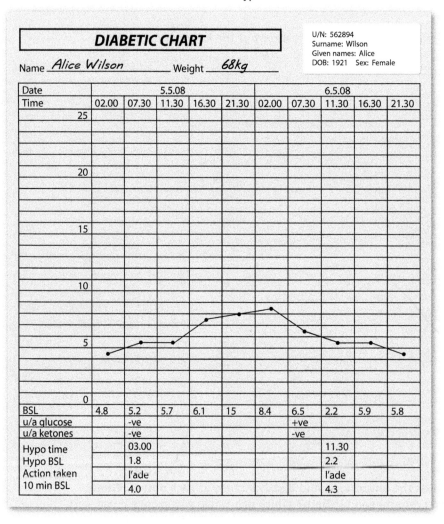

DIABETIC CHART

U/N: 562894
Surname: Wilson
Given names: Alice
DOB: 1921   Sex: Female

Name *Alice Wilson*   Weight *68kg*

Date		5.5.08					6.5.08			
Time	02.00	07.30	11.30	16.30	21.30	02.00	07.30	11.30	16.30	21.30
BSL	4.8	5.2	5.7	6.1	15	8.4	6.5	2.2	5.9	5.8
u/a glucose		-ve					+ve			
u/a ketones		-ve					-ve			
Hypo time		03.00						11.30		
Hypo BSL		1.8						2.2		
Action taken		l'ade						l'ade		
10 min BSL		4.0						4.3		

b ▶4.5 **Listen to Peter, the Ward Nurse, handing over Alice Wilson to Christie, a nurse on the next shift, and mark the following statements True (T) or False (F).**

1 Mrs Wilson has been having a few hypos lately.
2 She is 95 years old.
3 She's having insulin to try and stabilise her.
4 She's on qds plus 2 am BSL.
5 Her blood sugar levels should be between 4 and 8 mmols before meals.
6 Her blood sugar levels should go over 10 mmols half an hour after a meal.
7 Alice is still eating the wrong types of food.
8 Her BSL went up to 25 in the evening.
9 The Dietitian and Diabetes Educator will both visit Alice.
10 Alice has not had a hypoglycaemic attack today.

c ▶4.5 **Listen again and correct any mistakes on Alice's chart on page 36.**

d **Based on her chart, how would you describe Alice's diabetes?**

e **In pairs, practise handing over Alice Wilson. Student A, you are Peter; Student B, you are Christie. Use the corrected chart on page 36. Swap roles and practise again.**

Share your knowledge

In small groups, discuss the following questions and then feed back your group's ideas to the class.

- Diabetes management is especially important for elderly patients. What sort of information do they need?
- What co-morbidities (diseases that exist at the same time as another illness) in the elderly might make diabetes management more difficult?
- How could you best help an elderly patient with diabetes management?

UNIT 5 Medical specimens

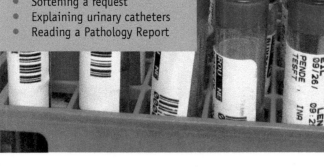
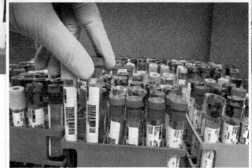

- Explaining pathology tests
- Asking for clarification
- Checking understanding
- Telephone skills: contacting other staff
- Explaining renal failure
- Softening a request
- Explaining urinary catheters
- Reading a Pathology Report

Explaining pathology tests

1 a In pairs, discuss the following questions.

1 Are you familiar with the Pathology department in hospital? What kinds of test are done there?
2 Why is it important for nurses to understand the results of pathology tests?

b ▶5.1 Listen to a conversation between Mrs Faisal, a patient, and Frances, the Ward Nurse, and answer the following questions.

1 What symptoms does Mrs Faisal have?
2 What condition might she have?
3 What is the name of the test which will be performed at Pathology?
4 What does Frances have to collect from the patient?

Communication focus: asking for clarification

2 a In pairs, discuss the following questions.

- If you were unsure of an instruction or some information, how would you ask for clarification in English?
- Why is it important to clarify any instructions you don't understand?

b ▶5.1 Listen again. Match the extracts (1–5) to the responses (a–e).

1 It burns when I go to the toilet, and I have to go all the time.	a Yes, the sample is less likely to have bacteria …
2 Is that right?	b Yes. It hurts when the urine comes out, …
3 What was it?	c Right. So what you're saying is that it hurts when you're actually passing urine …
4 He'll want you to do a urine specimen …	d Its full name is *urinary tract infection*.
5 Less contamination?	e OK. So you want me to do a urine specimen, do you?

c   Complete the following clarification strategies using the words in the box.

intonation   repeat   paraphrase   clarify

1   _____ the information back to the speaker.
2   _____ what has been said.
3   Use a questioning _____ pattern.
4   Ask the speaker to _____ what they have said.

d   In pairs, practise using the clarification strategies to respond to the following sentences.
   • I've got a lot of problems when I go to the toilet.
   • It burns when I go to the toilet.
   • I have to go to the toilet all of the time.
   • You might have a urinary tract infection.
   • The doctor will want you to do a urine specimen.
   • There's less contamination with a midstream specimen.

e   In pairs, practise giving information and asking for clarification. Student A, you are Frances; Student B, you are Mrs Faisal. Remember to use the clarification strategies. Swap roles and practise again.

Share your knowledge

In small groups, discuss the following questions and then feed back your group's ideas to the class.
   • How do you ensure privacy for your patients?
   • What cultural issues are important in providing privacy?
   • When might a patient request a chaperone?

Communication focus: checking understanding

3   a   ▶5.2 Listen to the rest of the conversation between Mrs Faisal and Frances, and put the following extracts in the correct order.
   ☐ Try to catch the middle part of the urine stream.
   ☐ You need to clean the area around the urethra from front to back with these disposable wipes.
   ☐ Tighten the lid before you give me the specimen container, please.
   ☐ Don't touch the inside of the container when you take the lid off.
   ☐ Wash your hands thoroughly.

b   Frances uses several strategies to check understanding. Match the strategies (1–4) to the expressions from the dialogue (a–d).

1 Ask the patient to repeat the information back to you	a Could you repeat back the steps for me so I can be sure you followed my explanation?
2 Ask the patient to demonstrate the use of the equipment	b Do you understand/see what I mean?
3 Ask for clarification to ensure the patient understands what has been said	c Can you show me how you'll hold the specimen jar?
4 Ask the patient to list the steps of a procedure or process	d Right, so step one is?

c In pairs, practise asking for and giving instructions for a midstream urine specimen (MSU). Student A, you are a nurse; Student B, you are a patient. Remember to use the strategies for clarification and checking understanding. Swap roles and practise again.

Telephone skills: contacting other staff

4 a In pairs, discuss the following questions.

1 What hospital communication systems are you familiar with?
2 What do you think are the features of a good communication system?
3 How is technology changing the way we communicate in the workplace?

b ▶5.3 Listen to a telephone conversation between Frances and Dr Sinclair, an SHO, and mark the following statements True (T) or False (F).

1 Frances calls Dr Sinclair to check on the results of Mrs Faisal's urine test.
2 Dr Sinclair asks Frances to remind her about Mrs Faisal's diagnosis.
3 The doctor has decided not to prescribe antibiotics.
4 A midstream urine specimen has been collected from the patient but the nurse needs the doctor to sign a Pathology Form.

c ▶5.3 Listen to the conversation again and complete the following extract.

Frances: It's Frances from eight west here. I'm (1) _____calling_____ _____about_____ one of your patients, Mrs Faisal.

Dr Sinclair: Er, Mrs Faisal? Can you (2) _____ _____ ?

Frances: Yeah, she was admitted two days ago, er ...

Dr Sinclair: Yeah, I remember. Isn't she (3) _____ _____ the removal of an ovarian cyst?

Frances: Yeah, that's the patient. I think she may have a UTI. She's (4) _____ _____ frequency, urgency and pain when she passes urine.

Dr Sinclair: Right. Is she (5) _____ ?

Frances: Yeah, her temp's (6) _____ _____ _____ . She's around thirty-seven point eight. She doesn't feel brilliant either – general (7) _____ .

Dr Sinclair: ... Can you take an (8) _____ and I'll come over and (9) _____ _____ some antibiotics.

Frances: The MSU's already done, but I'll leave the (10) _____ _____ at the desk to be signed. Then we can send it to Pathology...

d In pairs, practise the telephone conversation. Student A, you are Frances; Student B, you are Dr Sinclair. Remember to use the strategies for clarification and checking understanding. Swap roles and practise again.

Medical focus: the kidneys

5 **a** **In pairs, discuss the following questions.**

- How important is the role of the kidneys in our overall health?
- Have you had experience of caring for a patient with a kidney problem? If so, how did you manage his/her condition?

b **Read the patient information leaflet and answer the following questions.**

1 What are the functions of the kidneys?
2 What are the filtration units of the kidney called?
3 Which part of the kidney controls salt and water concentration levels?
4 Which part of the urinary system stores urine?
5 What is the tube that carries urine outside the body called?

How do your kidneys work?

Unfiltered blood enters the kidney for filtration through the renal artery from the heart. Blood passes to the kidneys in large quantities so that it can be filtered well and have most of the waste products removed. Renal veins carry the cleaned blood away from each kidney. Renal veins are wider than renal arteries because they transport blood towards the inferior vena cava of the heart. The blood returned from the heart through the renal artery contains a toxic product, called urea, and also high levels of salt and large amounts of water. The kidney's function is to filter out these unwanted materials. In addition, the kidney also reabsorbs any products the body needs and secretes waste materials as urine.

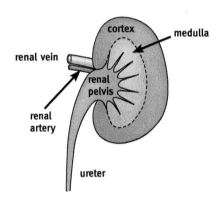

Blood enters the kidney through the hard outer layer, or cortex. The filtration units of the kidney, called nephrons, are found in the renal cortex. The nephrons help to filter out waste from the blood, leaving a filtrate of important salts and glucose. The next section of the kidney is called the renal medulla. This is where the level of salt and water in urine is controlled. Sodium ions are concentrated in the medulla so that very concentrated urine is produced. Any excess water and waste products are then secreted as urine. The urine collects in the renal pelvis, which is the fan-shaped section at the narrowest part of the kidney that joins onto each ureter. The ureters are the two tubes which transport the urine from the kidney to the bladder, or storage section. From the bladder there is another tube called the urethra which is where the urine passes to the outside.

c **In pairs, practise explaining how the kidneys work. First, use the information leaflet to help you. Then try using just the diagram of the kidney. Swap roles and practise again.**

Explaining renal failure

6 **a** Match the medical terms (1–13) to their meanings (a–m).

1 urinalysis	a the measurement of how acidic or alkaline a solution is
2 urine	b a toileting receptacle which is used by bed-bound patients
3 urinal	c a sample, usually of urine or blood
4 bed pan	d protein in the urine, also called *albuminuria*
5 renal	e the process of analysing urine using physical or chemical tests
6 pH	f blood in the urine
7 proteinuria	g also called *bottle*; used by male patients to pass urine into
8 haematuria (US hematuria)	h relating to the kidneys
9 specimen	i the fluid which is excreted by the kidneys
10 oedema	j no urine output
11 anuria	k excessive accumulation of fluid in the tissues
12 nephrons	l low urine output
13 oliguria	m filtering units of the kidney

b Underline the stressed syllable in words 1–13.

c In pairs, take turns to say a word and ask your partner to explain it.

d ▶5.4 Mr Zelnic has been admitted to the renal ward for renal function tests. He has been passing blood in his urine for the past two weeks and has lower back pain. Listen to the conversation between Everson, the Ward Nurse, and Mr Zelnic. Mark the following statements True (T) or False (F).

1 In kidney disease, there is a build-up of toxic waste products in the blood.
2 Oliguria is a symptom of end stage renal failure.
3 Fluid retention indicates that the filtration system of the kidneys has failed.
4 End stage renal failure can be treated.
5 The symptoms of kidney disease appear immediately.

e ▶5.4 Listen again and complete the following extracts using the words in the box.

toxic	oedema	nephrons	renal failure	~~renal~~	urine	lethargic	renal transplant

1 If the kidneys stop working properly, _____renal_____ , or kidney, disease could be the result.
2 If the _____ don't filter properly, the waste products aren't removed.
3 Eventually, _____ levels of waste products build up in the blood.
4 Oliguria can be a symptom of the early stage of _____ .
5 If the kidney disease is untreated, the nephrons stop working altogether and no _____ is passed at all.
6 Because your kidneys are not filtering out waste products or excess water, your hands or feet may swell; this build-up of fluid is called _____ .
7 You may also feel _____ because your blood hasn't been cleaned and can't function properly.
8 People with end stage renal failure have to go on dialysis or perhaps even have a _____ .

Communication focus: softening a request

7 a ▶5.5 **Listen to the rest of the conversation between Everson and Mr Zelnic and answer the following questions.**

1 What kind of specimen is needed for urinalysis?
2 What three things can the urinalysis check for?

b Look at the following sentences. Are these the same as sentences you heard in the conversation between Everson and Mr Zelnic? If not, which words are missing?

1 I'd like you to do it now, if that's all right.
2 I need an ordinary sample of urine.
3 It takes a few minutes to get a reading.
4 I'm checking for proteinuria; that means protein in the urine.
5 Ring when you want me to collect it.

c ▶5.6 **Listen to the sentences with the words missing.**

d ▶5.7 **Now listen to the sentences with the words included. How does adding the missing words soften the request?**

e In pairs, practise explaining the urinalysis test. Student A, you are Everson; Student B, you are Mr Zelnic. Remember to use the strategies for clarification and checking understanding, and to soften instructions appropriately. Swap roles and practise again.

Explaining urinary catheters

Short-term urinary catheters may be inserted in patients who have urinary retention, or have restricted movement which does not allow them to get up to the toilet easily. Long-term urinary catheters are used for patients who are permanently incontinent.

8 a In pairs, discuss the following questions.

1 Are you familiar with the use of urinary catheters?
2 What other types of patient might require urinary catheters?
3 What are some of the complications that can occur with catheterisation?
4 Are you aware of any new procedures/developments in catheterisation?

b ▶5.8 **Listen to a conversation between Mrs Kastel, a patient, and Jo, her nurse, and answer the following questions.**

1 What is Mrs Kastel complaining of?
2 What is Jo going to do to relieve Mrs Kastel's problem?
3 What is used to collect the urine?

c Complete the following definitions.

1 Urinary retention is when a patient can't _____ _____ .
2 An indwelling catheter (IDC) is a tube which is left _____ _____ , or in place.
3 Aseptic technique keeps equipment sterile to avoid _____ .
4 A catheter drainage bag is a _____ bag which collects the urine that drains out of the urinary catheter.

d ▶5.8 **The nurse and patient both use strategies for clarification by rephrasing information. Listen again and match the original information (1−6) to the rephrased version (a−f).**

1 I haven't been able to use this bedpan at all.
2 You've still got some urinary retention after your operation, haven't you?
3 I might have to put in a catheter to drain the urine.
4 ... a tube which is left in situ −
5 And you have to take care how you put the tube in so I don't get an infection.
6 The catheter bag you're talking about is one of these.

a Is that the tube which goes into your bladder?
b That's exactly it. It's called aseptic technique because it keeps equipment sterile to avoid contamination.
c I mean, left in place.
d You mean that you haven't been able to pass any urine?
e It's a transparent bag which collects the urine that drains out of the catheter.
f You mean that I can't go to the toilet?

e **In pairs, practise explaining an IDC. Student A, you are a nurse; Student B, you are a patient complaining of urinary retention. Swap roles and practise again.**

Charting and documentation: Pathology Report

Pathology Reports are usually sent to the ward via the hospital intranet. A paper copy is also sent to the ward and filed in the patient's notes as a permanent record.

9 a In pairs, discuss the following questions.

1 Are you familiar with Pathology Reports?
2 What sort of information do they contain?
3 When do nurses refer to them?
4 Are you familiar with Pathology Reports online, i.e. on the hospital intranet?
5 When would a nurse phone a patient's doctor about a pathology result?

b In pairs, look at the Pathology Report on page 45 and answer the following questions.

1 What information does this Pathology Report contain?
2 What test was performed?
3 What type of specimen was collected?
4 What time was the specimen collected?
5 When was the specimen analysed in the lab?
6 What did the pathologist notice under the microscope?
7 What do you think *proteus mirabilis* is the name of?
8 What kind of drugs are ampicillin, cephalexin, trimethoprim and nitrofurantoin?
9 What comment did the pathologist make about Mrs Chu's specimen?

Pathology Report
Name: Gloria Chu

Lab No: 4524368   Micro No: GC06M74
Collected: 18:45   6-Mar-08
Urine microbiology
Registered: 07:18   7-Mar-08
Specimen: MSU
Ward of collection: 16E

Microscopy:

Leucocytes	40	x 10^6 / LRR (<10)
Erythrocytes	20	x 10^6 / LRR (<10)
Other		bacteria 1+

Antimicrobials: Not detected

Culture: *Proteus mirabilis > 10^8/L*

Ampicillin	**Sensitive**
Cephalexin	**Sensitive**
Trimethoprim	**Sensitive**
Nitrofurantoin	**Sensitive**

Comment: Possible UTI

C   **Complete the following explanations using the words in the box.**

pathology	antimicrobial	erythrocytes	culture
microbiology	microscopy	bacteria	sensitive
microbes	~~leucocytes~~		

1   Elevated _leucocytes_ , or white blood cells, can indicate infection.
2   The bacteria in Mrs Chu's urine is _____ to ampicillin, so she started treatment with the antibiotic this morning.
3   The presence of _____ in the urine strongly suggests that Mrs Chu has a UTI.
4   _____ , which include viruses and bacteria, are infective agents.
5   Medications which attack microbes in the body are called _____ drugs.
6   The study of micro-organisms – that is, organisms which cannot be seen by the naked eye – is called _____ .
7   Red blood cells, also called _____ , transport oxygen in the blood.
8   The study of diseases is called _____ .
9   _____ is the use of a microscope to visualise the presence of microbes in specimens.
10   The population of microbes which is grown in a laboratory and analysed by a pathologist is called a _____ .

Share your knowledge

1   Why is it important to identify the organism which causes infection?
2   Why is the overuse of antibiotics a problem?
3   What is MRSA and what can it cause?
4   Is MRSA a problem in your country?

UNIT 6 Medications

- Administering medication
- Doing a medication check
- Working as part of a team
- Checking medication orders for accuracy
- Explaining drug interactions
- Checking the 'five rights' of medication administration
- Reading a Prescription Chart

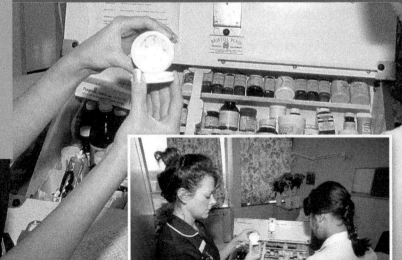

Administering medication

The use of controlled drugs (CDs) is regulated by legislation. The legislation sets out rules for the safekeeping of controlled drugs, the records which must be kept, and the manner of administering controlled drugs.

1 a In pairs, discuss the following questions.

1 What is your experience of administering controlled drugs?
2 What is your experience of drug prescriptions?
3 What rules relating to the administration of controlled drugs are there in your country?
4 Why are controlled drugs regulated so strictly?

b ▶6.1 Natasha, a Ward Nurse, needs to give her patient, Mr Song, an injection, and she is looking for a nurse to help her. Listen to the conversations and answer the following questions.

1 Why does Natasha need assistance?
2 What medication is Natasha going to give Mr Song?
3 Why can't Marek help her?
4 Is Anna able to help?

c Natasha asks for the assistance of other nurses. Match the beginnings (1–4) to the endings (a–d). Sometimes more than one answer is possible.

1 Have you	a free at the moment?
2 Are you	b checking this morphine with me, please?
3 Are you	c got a minute? I just need a drug check.
4 Would you mind	d busy at the moment or can you do a drug check with me?

d ▶6.1 **Listen again and check your answers. Then match the questions in Exercise 1c to the correct responses (a–d).**

a   Sorry, Natasha, I'm tied up at the moment.
b   Oh sorry, Natasha, I can't at the moment. I'm just in the middle of something, and I can't leave it.
c   Yes, sure. Let me just wash my hands and I'll be with you.
d   I will be in a minute.

e **Complete the following extracts using the words in the box. What do all the expressions mean?**

snowed   flat out   eyeballs   run off

1   No, sorry. I'm up to my _____ in work.
2   I'd love to help, but I'm _____ under.
3   I can't. I'm _____ at the moment.
4   Actually, I'm _____ my feet.

f **In pairs, practise asking for assistance with a drug check, using Exercises 1c–e as a guide. Swap roles and practise again.**

Doing a medication check

2 a ▶6.2 **Natasha and Anna have gone to the Treatment Room to get some medication for Mr Song. Listen to the conversation and answer the following questions.**

1   Which drug has the doctor prescribed for Mr Song?
2   Why does Natasha ask Anna to get the drug from the drug cupboard?
3   What do they have to do when they take the ampoules from the cupboard?
4   What do they have to do in the drug book?
5   What information does Natasha show Anna on the ampoule?

b ▶6.2 **Listen again and put the following steps in the correct order.**

☐ Check the number of ampoules left in the cupboard
☐ Draw up the correct amount of the drug in a syringe
☐ Check the expiry date of the drug in the ampoule
☐ Check the time the last injection was given to the patient
☒ Check the drug order in the Medication Chart
☐ Sign and witness the drug book
☐ Check the amount of drug drawn up in the syringe
☐ Get an ampoule from the locked cupboard

c **In pairs, try to remember the order of the steps in a medication check without looking at Exercise 2b.**

d Match the strategies for correct administration of a medication (1–6) to the rationales (a–f).

1 Anna checks that the drug count is correct before checking out an ampoule of pethidine for Mr Song.	a Out-of-date drugs may not be effective.
2 Natasha checks the prescription in the Prescription Chart with Anna.	b This ensures that none of the ampoules have been taken and misused.
3 Natasha and Anna check the ampoule together.	c This is to prove that the syringe contains the controlled drug, not another colourless liquid.
4 Natasha and Anna check the expiry date on the ampoule.	d This ensures that the correct drug and dose is checked out.
5 Natasha draws up the correct amount of the drug in the syringe and shows Anna.	e This proves that the patient has received the controlled drug.
6 Anna watches Natasha give Mr Song the injection of pethidine.	f Controlled drugs may only be given with a written order.

e In pairs, practise assisting with a drug check. Student A, you are Natasha; Student B, you are Anna. Use Exercise 2b as a guide. Swap roles and practise again.

Communication focus: working as part of a team

There are many occasions when teamwork is critical in the healthcare environment.

3 Match the strategies for working as part of a team (1–6) to the examples (a–f).

1 Ask for assistance politely	a Thanks for helping me, Hans. It was much easier to do this together.
2 Share the workload	b – Mrs Cho is refusing to drink anything. I don't know what to do. – Have you tried apple juice? I know she'll drink that.
3 Acknowledge the contribution of other staff	c Would you mind giving me a hand? I need someone to check this medication.
4 Provide alternative suggestions	d I'm really snowed under at the moment. Can anyone else help you?
5 Be an active part of a team rather than work as an individual	e I've finished all my work. Does anyone need a hand?
6 Recognise when you're unable to help	f Do you mind taking beds one and two, and I'll take three and four?

Share your knowledge

In small groups, discuss the following questions and then feed back your group's ideas to the class.

1 What do you understand by the term *team nursing*?
2 What are some advantages of team nursing?
3 What arc some disadvantages of team nursing?
4 What nursing styles are you familiar with or have worked under (for example, holistic nursing, primary care nursing, task oriented nursing)?

Checking medication orders for accuracy

Some medications must be checked by two nurses before being given to the patient. It may also be necessary to check the result of a blood test before the medication can be given. In the following case, the patient has had a blood test to check the International Normalised Ratio (INR). The INR measures the time it takes for a blood clot to form in the body.

4 a **In pairs, discuss the following questions.**
   1 What sort of medications need to be checked by two nurses, and why?
   2 Why do some medications require a blood test before being given?

   b ▶6.3 **Josh and Susanna, two Ward Nurses, are checking a medication together. Listen to the conversation and answer the following questions.**
   1 What does Josh want Susanna to do?
   2 Who is the medication for?
   3 What kind of medication is it?
   4 What result do the nurses check before giving the medication?
   5 Who signs the Prescription Chart?

   c ▶6.3 **Put the following stages of Josh and Susanna's medication check in the correct order. Listen again and check your answers.**
   ☐ Check the medication label
   ☐ Crosscheck chart and patient information
   ☐ Check the INR result
   ☐ Sign Medication Chart
   ☐ Crosscheck route
   ☒ Ask for help
   ☐ Crosscheck dose on Medication Chart
   ☐ Take out medication
   ☐ Countersign Medication Chart
   ☐ Crosscheck time of administration

   d **Mrs Egerts in bed 6 has been prescribed warfarin 5mg to be taken orally. In pairs, practise checking medication orders. Student A, you are Josh; Student B, you are Susanna. Remember to crosscheck all of the information. Swap roles and practise again.**

Share your knowledge

In small groups, discuss the following questions and then feed back your group's ideas to the class.
1 Do you follow the same procedures for checking medication in your country?
2 If not, what procedure do you follow?
3 What are the advantages and disadvantages of having a single designated nurse for the medication round?

Medical focus: the metabolism of medication

Patient education in medication safety

Mr Albiston has just been prescribed atorvastatin to lower the levels of cholesterol in his blood. In order to ensure the safe usage of the medication when Mr Albiston returns home, Helen, the Ward Nurse, is going to talk to him about his medication.

5 a **In pairs, discuss the following questions.**

1 Why is patient education about medications an important role for nurses?
2 What are some of the risks of self-medication?
3 What sort of things might a nurse discuss with a patient regarding a new medication?

b ▶6.4 **Listen to the conversation between Helen and Mr Albiston and mark the following statements True (T) or False (F).**

1 Atorvastatin is used for patients with low cholesterol levels.
2 The medication stops atherosclerosis in the arteries.
3 The drug is absorbed in the liver.
4 Atorvastatin blocks the enzyme which causes the liver to make cholesterol.
5 It doesn't matter what time of day atorvastatin is taken.

c ▶6.4 **The diagram below shows the absorption and metabolism of atorvastatin. Listen again and complete the following patient information leaflet.**

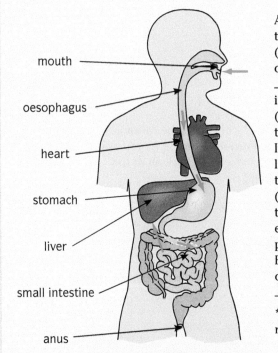

mouth

oesophagus

heart

stomach

liver

small intestine

anus

After you swallow the tablet, it (1) ___enters___ the gastrointestinal tract, or GIT*. It (2) _____ _____ the oesophagus, the tube which (3) _____ _____ the stomach. The tablet passes into your stomach, where it is absorbed. It (4) _____ _____ the liquids there so it can pass into your bloodstream. It then (5) _____ _____ the liver (6) _____ the small intestine, the part under the stomach. The drug is (7) _____ , or chemically changed, in the liver. The liver stops the production of an enzyme which (8) _____ the body to produce a harmful type of cholesterol. By (9) _____ this enzyme, the amount of 'bad cholesterol' which is (10) _____ _____ the blood is reduced.

* a series of organs of the digestive system which runs from the mouth to the anus

d **In pairs, practise explaining the metabolism of medication. Student A, you are a nurse; Student B, you are a patient. Use the diagram in Exercise 5c to help you. Swap roles and practise again.**

Explaining drug interactions

6 a Read the information leaflet about atorvastatin interactions and answer the following questions.

1 What drugs are contraindicated (not advisable) with atorvastatin?
2 Why would decreased elimination of atorvastatin be problematic?
3 What other things are contraindicated?

b Complete the following precautions using the phrases in the box.

> should/must not be taken   are warned not
> increases the toxic effects
> precaution to take   ~~advised not to~~
> should be   must not take   increasing the risk

1 You are _advised not to_____ drink alcohol with the medication, as this can increase the risk of liver disease.
2 The medication _____ with drugs such as the antibiotic erythromycin and cyclosporine, as these reduce the elimination of atorvastatin from the body, _____ of muscle damage.
3 No statins _____ combined with niacin (nicotinic acid).
4 You _____ warfarin and atorvastatin together as this increases the anticoagulant properties of warfarin.
5 Atorvastatin _____ with grapefruit juice as this stops a vital enzyme from working and _____ of the drug.
6 Not eating citrus fruit related to grapefruit is an important _____ to avoid side effects.

c *Adverse events relating to medications are a significant and costly problem in hospitals. Several strategies have been introduced to Best Practice which aim to reduce medication errors. One such strategy is the use of pharmacists for consultation and review of medication charts at ward level. Pharmacists usually visit the ward once a week.*

▶ **6.5 Listen to a conversation between Helen, a Ward Nurse, and Sonia, the hospital Pharmacist, and answer the following questions.**

1 What is Sonia doing?
2 What is she speaking to Helen about?
3 Why is Sonia concerned?
4 What is nicotinic acid also known as?
5 What action will Helen take?

Atorvastatin interactions

Atorvastatin should not be combined with drugs which decrease its elimination from the body. For example, drugs such as the antibiotic erythromycin and the anti-rejection drug cyclosporine.

Concurrent use of atorvastatin and erythromycin could increase levels of the atorvastatin in the body and increase the risk of muscle damage.

Statins should not be combined with niacin (nicotinic acid), often sold as an over-the-counter medication to lower cholesterol and present in multivitamin tablets.

Atorvastatin increases the anticoagulant effect of warfarin, so patients taking atorvastatin and warfarin together should be monitored carefully.

Statins may cause liver disease, such as jaundice, so it is necessary to monitor liver function. Alcoholic beverages must be limited or avoided.

Large quantities of grapefruit juice (more than 1.2 litres daily) should not be taken. Grapefruit juice inhibits an intestinal enzyme whose function it is to break down and absorb medications. When this enzyme is blocked, the blood level of the drug increases, and toxic side effects from the medication may be felt.

Fruit related to grapefruit, such as Seville oranges (often used in marmalade), should also be avoided.

d ▶6.5 **Listen again and complete the following extracts.**

1   I had a talk to him about some things he'll _____ _____
    _____ careful of at home.
2   ... when he started atorvastatin. _____ _____ _____
    _____ about something he was started on today.
3   He _____ _____ taking that with atorvastatin.
4   He _____ _____ Vitamin B3 – I mean, nicotinic acid – on its
    own or in any other preparation.
5   Does he know _____ _____ drink grapefruit juice with the
    atorvastatin?

e   **In pairs, practise explaining the interactions of atorvastatin. Student A, you
    are a nurse; Student B, you are a patient who has just been prescribed the
    drug for the first time. Swap roles and practise again.**

Charting and documentation: Prescription Chart

7   a   **Sonia, the hospital Pharmacist, has just checked Mr Albiston's Prescription
    Chart on her regular ward visit. In pairs, look at the chart on page 88 and
    discuss the following questions.**

1   What kind of chart is it?
2   Are you familiar with this style of chart?
3   What sort of information is on the chart?
4   Who is responsible for recording information on the chart?
5   How often is new information added to the chart?

b   **The following abbreviations are all commonly used on Prescription Charts.
    Match the abbreviations (1–10) to their meanings (a–j).**

1 tab.	a injection given into the subcutaneous layer of the skin
2 cap.	b at night
3 mg	c injection given into the muscle
4 mcg	d milligram – unit of mass which is 1/1000 of a gram
5 ml	e millilitre – unit of volume which is 1/1000 of a litre
6 po	f gelatine-coated medication
7 sc	g microgram – unit of mass which is 1/1000 of a milligram
8 IM	h solid medication, also called a *pill*
9 mane	i from the Latin *per os*: by mouth
10 nocte	j in the morning

c   **Which of the abbreviations in Exercise 7b are found on the Prescription
    Chart on page 88?**

d   **In pairs, take turns to ask for the meaning of an abbreviation.**

e   **In pairs, look at the chart on page 88 again and answer the following questions.**

1   When was Mr Albiston ordered atorvastatin?
2   What time does he have to take the medication?
3   Has he already started taking the medication?
4   What new medication was Mr Albiston ordered on 28 April?
5   Has he already been given this medication?
6   Would you give Mr Albiston the medication ordered on 28 April?

Checking the 'five rights' of medication administration

8   a   **In pairs, look at the 'five rights' and discuss the following questions.**

- Are these the same medication checks which are performed in your country?
- If not, how are they different?
- How would you check them?

The 'five rights'

1	The right drug	☐
2	The right patient	☐
3	The right dose	☐
4	The right route	☐
5	The right time	☐

b   ▶6.6 **Beatriz, a Student Nurse, is doing a medication assessment with Jo, a Registered Nurse. Listen to the conversation and mark the order that Beatriz checks the five rights in.**

c   **Match the 'rights' (1–5) to their meanings (a–e).**

1 The right drug	a Check the route of administration on the Prescription Chart
2 The right patient	b Check how often the medication is to be given and at what times
3 The right dose	c Crosscheck the name of the medication on the Prescription Chart and the medication label
4 The right route	d Crosscheck the dose of the medication on the Prescription Chart and on the medication label
5 The right time	e Check the patient's full name by checking the hospital label on the Prescription Chart and by checking the patient's identity bracelet; also check the patient's date of birth if necessary

d   **In pairs, practise doing nurse–nurse medication checks. Look at Mrs Gupta's Prescription Chart on page 87. Ask questions about the medication administration, following the five rights. Swap roles and practise again.**

Share your knowledge

In small groups, discuss the following questions and then feed back your group's ideas to the class.

- Do you have Nurse Prescribers in your country?
- What do you think are the advantages and disadvantages of having Nurse Prescribers?

- Reviewing IV infusions
- Passing on instructions to colleagues
- Assessing IV cannulas
- Telephone skills: taking a message about patient care
- Checking IV orders
- Charting fluid intake and output

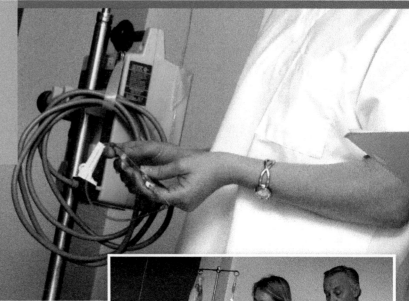

Reviewing IV infusions

IV infusions are treated in the same way as medications. They must be prescribed by a doctor on an IV Prescription Chart. IV Prescription Charts only remain current for 24 hours, so doctors must review IV infusion regimes daily.

1 a **In pairs, discuss the following questions.**

    1 What is your experience of IV therapy?
    2 When might a patient require IV therapy?
    3 What IV therapy equipment are you familiar with?

  b **In pairs, look at the picture and discuss the following questions.**

    1 What equipment can you see?
    2 What do you think they are discussing?

  c ▶ **7.1 Dr Venturi has come to the ward to review his patients' IV infusion regimes. Listen to the first part of his conversation with Paula, the Ward Nurse, and mark the following statements True (T) or False (F).**

    1 Doctor Venturi wants to review Mrs Boland's IV fluids.
    2 Paula is looking after Mrs Boland all day today.
    3 Mrs Dillip's potassium levels are above average.
    4 Mrs Dillip has been started on one litre of Normal Saline over eight hours.
    5 Her antibiotics are to be given through a separate line.
    6 Mr Claussen's cannula will have to be resited before he goes home.

d ▶7.1 **Listen again and circle the words or abbreviations (a or b) you hear.**

1 a intravenous fluids
   (b) IV fluids
2 a cannula
   b IVC
3 a potassium
   b K
4 a Normal Saline
   b N/S
5 a millimols
   b mmols
6 a potassium chloride
   b KCl
7 a IV antibiotics
   b IV ABs

e ▶7.1 **Listen again and tick which instructions you hear.**

1 ☐ Could you change Mrs Boland's IV line when the infusion has gone through, please?
   ☐ Could you take down Mrs Boland's IV when it's finished, please?
2 ☐ Leave it (the cannula) for another day ...
   ☐ Leave the infusion up for another day.
3 ☐ Could you start her on a litre of Normal Saline with 40 millimols of KCl?
   ☐ Could you take down the litre of Normal Saline and put up a Normal Saline with 40 millimols of KCl?
4 ☐ Can you run it over six hours, please?
   ☐ Can you run it over eight hours, please?
5 ☐ Can you leave the cannula in for his antibiotics, please?
   ☐ Can you take out his cannula before he goes home, please?

Passing on instructions to colleagues

2 **a** *Paula makes notes of Dr Venturi's orders so that she can pass them on to Suzy when she returns.*

   ▶7.2 **Listen to the second part of the conversation and write B for Mrs Boland, D for Mrs Dillip, and C for Mr Claussen next to the information in Paula's notes which relates to them.**

   b **Why did Paula put a tick next to three of the instructions in her notes?**

   Notes for Suzy
   Ⓓ Cannula inserted ✓   ☐ Leave cannula
   ☐ Light dressing ✓   ☐ K levels
   ☐ Take down IV when   ☐ Home this pm
      thr.   ☐ Put up IL N/S with KCl
   ☐ Run IV 8°   40 mmols
   ☐ IV ABs   ☐ Cannula out ✓

c ▶7.2 **Listen again and write down what Paula says to pass on the instructions.**

1   Take down IV when thr.
    He asked if you could take the IV down when it's run through.

2   Leave cannula
    _____

3   Put up 1L N/S with KCl 40 mmols
    _____

4   Run IV 8°
    _____

5   Cannula out
    _____

d   **Dr Venturi has completed his rounds and has left instructions for two patients. Student A, read the notes on page 88 and pass on the message to your colleague, Student B. Student B, read the notes on page 93 and pass on the message to Student A.**

> ## Share your knowledge
>
> **In small groups, discuss the following questions and then feed back your group's ideas to the class.**
>
> 1   What protocols do you follow for checking IV infusions?
> 2   What protocols do you follow for the care of IV cannulas?
> 3   Do you use preloaded IV infusions – IV infusions which already include additives; for example, Normal Saline with 40 mmols KCl – in your country, or do you load the additives before administering the infusion?
> 4   What are the advantages and disadvantages of preloaded infusion bags?

Medical focus: IV cannulas

Assessing IV cannulas

3 a ▶7.3 **Listen to a conversation between Mrs Boxmeer, who is waiting for her next IV infusion, and Angela, a Ward Nurse who is inspecting the IV cannula site, and answer the following questions.**

1   Why does Angela check the insertion site of Mrs Boxmeer's IV?
2   What signs of infection does the nurse check for?
3   How many more doses of IV antibiotics does Mrs Boxmeer have?
4   What is the problem with the location of Mrs Boxmeer's cannula?
5   What happens at the first sign of infection?

b Match the medical terms (1–9) to their meanings (a–i).

1 nosocomial	a describes an IV line which stops running because the line becomes blocked off due to patient movement
2 phlebitis	b redness of the skin which can indicate infection
3 infiltration	c contracted in hospital; from the Greek *noso-*, meaning *disease*
4 Staph	d replace in a different vein
5 IV giving set	e staphylococci bacteria – types of microbes which are usually found on the skin
6 erythema	f inflammation of the vein; from the Greek *phleb-*, meaning *vein*
7 aseptic technique	g tubing which is spiked into the infusion bag and connected to the IV cannula; also called an IV administration set
8 resite an IV cannula	h *no touch* method used to avoid contamination
9 positional	i when fluid leaks into surrounding tissues; in nursing jargon: *tissued*

c Underline the stressed syllable in words 1–9.

d In pairs, take turns to say a word and ask your partner to define it.

e ▶7.3 Angela explains to Mrs Boxmeer what happens when an IV cannula needs to be replaced. Listen again and complete the following extracts.

1 Can I just check that your IV cannula is all right before I __put__ __up__ the next infusion?

2 I'll have a look on your Care Plan to see when the doctor _____ the IV _____ .

3 It means that I'll call the doctor to come and _____ _____ a new one.

4 I'll stop this drip now and _____ _____ your cannula.

5 Can't they _____ the cannula _____ ?

6 Sorry, you've still got six doses of IV antibiotics, so we need to _____ _____ a new line.

7 I hope they can find a more convenient spot to _____ it _____ .

8 The thing is that there is a lower risk of phlebitis if we _____ the cannula _____ your hand.

9 That's why we check the cannula site and _____ the cannula _____ at the first sign of infection.

10 Our hospital follows Evidence-Based Practice guidelines which suggest that we _____ IV cannulas _____ after seventy-two hours.

11 The number of days the IV is _____ _____ is recorded in the Care Plan.

Telephone skills: taking a message about patient care

The telephone is one of the main instruments of communication in the healthcare setting. Information about patient care is often given and received by phone or via phone messages, so it is very important that this is done accurately and clearly.

4 a In pairs, discuss the following questions.

1 Under what circumstances would nurses need to use the telephone to communicate information about patient care?

2 What sort of information would nurses receive by phone?

3 Have you experienced any difficulties taking messages over the phone? If so, what were they?

4 How can you avoid misunderstandings when taking phone messages?

b ▶ 7.4 Listen to a conversation between **Dr Gonzalez**, who has been paged about putting in a new cannula, and **Kasia**, the Ward Nurse who takes the message, and circle the details you hear.

Date of message	17 September 2008
Time of message	11.00hrs
Name of caller	Dr Gonzalez
Nature of call	Resite cannula Mrs Szubansky
Instructions	1 Michael to call Dr G re when cannula needs resite 2 Due time next IV ABs 3 Bleep Dr G on 645
Message documented in Patient Record	Yes / Not necessary
Signature of call recipient	K. Tolevskaya (RN)

c Look at the following guidelines for taking telephone messages. What did Kasia say in each case?

1 Make sure you have the details of the caller's identity.
   I'm sorry, I didn't hear your name properly. Who's calling, please?
2 Ask the caller to spell out any difficult names if you are unsure.
3 Make sure you understand the purpose of the call.
4 Stop the caller if s/he is giving the message too quickly for you to write it down.
5 Read the message back to the caller to confirm the details.
6 Let the caller know that you will pass the message on.
7 Ask for a contact number if the caller wants a return phone call.

d *Mr Henry is going to have a PICC line (Peripherally Inserted Central Catheter) in two days' time. He is having the special IV central line inserted because he has been prescribed long-term IV antibiotics. PICC lines do not have to be replaced every three days as standard cannulas do and so are more comfortable for the patient and have fewer infection risks.*

In pairs, practise giving and taking a telephone message. Student A, you are a nurse from the IV Infusion Room; use the notes on page 93. Student B, you are a Ward Nurse on Ward 16C; use the message pad on page 88. Use the guidelines for taking telephone messages. Swap roles and practise again.

Share your knowledge

In small groups, discuss the following questions and then feed back your group's ideas to the class.

1 In what other ways can messages be passed on?
2 How are messages passed on to other staff members in your workplace?
3 What are some of the problems which can occur when messages have to be passed on?

Charting and documentation: IV Prescription Chart

Checking IV orders

5 a **In pairs, look at the chart and discuss the following questions.**

1 What is this chart used for?
2 Are you familiar with this type of chart?

THE ALEXANDRA HOSPITAL

IV PRESCRIPTION CHART

Name of Patient: Mabyn Hadfield
U/N: 62388
DOB: 12.1.1920
Sex: Female

DRIP RATE CALCULATOR (1 Litre Bag) = Drops per Minute (DPM) Microdrip sets (60 drops = 1ml/hr) ml/hr = Drops/min

Time (hrs)	2	4	6	8	10	12	16	18	24
ml/hr (1L bag)	500	250	166	125	100	83	62	55	42
20 drop/ml set	167 DPM	83 DPM	55 DPM	42 DPM	33 DPM	28 DPM	21 DPM	18 DPM	14 DPM

Fluids must be prescribed daily – only one bag will be administered against each order

Year: 2009 — Medical Officer Prescription — Nursing Administration Record

Date / Time	Line Route	Volume	Fluid Type and Additive	Time to be infused	Dr Signature	Date Time start	Rate ml/hr	Nr 1 Nr 2	Time Stop	Volume Infused
30.05 01.00	IV	1000 ml	Normal Saline	8 hours	H.Khan	30.05 03.00	125 ml	G.L V.A	11.00	1000 ml
30.05 08.00	IV	1000 ml	5% Dextrose	10 hours	H.Khan	30.05 11.00	100 ml	C.A K.B		

---

b *Miss Mabyn Hadfield is an 89-year-old patient who was discovered on the kitchen floor of her flat by her neighbours. She had a fractured (broken) hip and was very dehydrated.*

▶**7.5 Listen to a conversation between two Ward Nurses, Cheryl and Karen, and answer the following questions.**

1 Why does Cheryl ask Karen to watch Miss Hadfield's IV?
2 Why did Miss Hadfield have the IV infusion to KVO (to keep the vein open) when she was admitted?
3 What IV solution does she have running at the moment?
4 What does Cheryl ask Karen to do?
5 What do Cheryl and Karen check on the IV Prescription Chart?
6 What two things do the nurses check on the IV Infusion Bag?
7 What does Cheryl have to work out before she puts up the IV infusion?
8 Who signs the IV Prescription Chart?
9 What information do the nurses check which is not recorded on the IV Prescription Chart?

c ▶7.5 Cheryl and Karen talk about concentration percentages, volumes and rates. Listen again and complete the following extract using the figures in the box.

30th	03.00	1000 ml	5%	16th	100 ml	5%	8
11.00	30th	11.00	10	1000 ml	ł	2010	

Cheryl: That's right. (1) __1__ litre of Normal Saline over (2) _____ hours. It went up at (3) _____ hours and it's through now at (4) _____ hours so I'll write that in here. And I'll write in the amount of (5) _____ . There. Now we can check out the next one. The date is (6) _____ of May, the route is IV and the fluid is (7) _____ Dextrose.

Karen: (8) _____ , yes, IV, yes, (9) _____ Dextrose, yes.

Cheryl: OK. We can check the IV infusion now. Here's the bag. I'll just show you. 5% Dextrose. It expires on the (10) _____ of July (11) _____ . Can you see the expiry date on the bag OK?

Karen: Yeah. 5% Dextrose, expires 16th of July, 2010. Correct.

Cheryl: Right, so let me write it in. 30th May, (12) _____ hours. The rate is one litre over (13) _____ hours. That's easy to work out. One litre – (14) _____ – divided by ten hours. That's (15) _____ an hour.

Charting fluid intake and output

When a patient is receiving IV therapy, it is important to keep an accurate record of the patient's fluid intake and output to avoid fluid overload.

6 a **In pairs, look at the chart on page 89 and discuss the following questions.**

1 Are you familiar with this type of chart?
2 What is it used for?
3 Who is responsible for filling out the chart?

b **Find abbreviations in the chart with the following meanings.**

1 Large amount Lge amt
2 Up to the toilet instead of using a bedpan or urinal so urine can be measured _____
3 Has had a bowel movement; bowels opened _____
4 Carried forward (an amount from a previous chart) _____
5 Urine output _____
6 Water _____
7 Bowels not opened _____
8 Small amount _____
9 Wet bed one plus (small amount) _____
10 Orange juice _____
11 To keep the vein open (for example, to administer IV antibiotics) _____
12 Aspirate (of a naso-gastric tube) _____
13 Moderate amount _____

c ▶7.6 **Miss Stavel, whose chart is on page 89, has been receiving IV therapy post-op after losing a lot of blood during an operation. Listen to a conversation between two night nurses, Rebecca and Casey, who are discussing Miss Stavel, and answer the following questions.**

1 What specifically are Rebecca and Casey discussing?
2 What is the problem?
3 What other information will they use to assess Miss Stavel's fluid status?
4 Circle the areas of the chart which the nurses are concerned about.

d ▶7.6 **Rebecca and Casey discuss a number of inaccuracies in the Fluid Balance Chart. Listen again and complete the following extracts using the words in the box.**

accuracy   point   inaccurately   mistakes   ~~record~~
record   recorded   measure   problem   properly

1 There's no __record__ of any intake from 10 am to 5 pm.
2 And at 5 pm they _____ the amount of water she drank
   _____ .
3 … they haven't been able to _____ it _____ every time.
4 There's also a _____ with the _____ of her urine output.
5 They can't have been able to measure her urine output with any
   _____ .
6 … there's no _____ adding up the intake and output because of the
   _____ …

e **Read the audioscript on page 103 and find what Rebecca and Casey say to point out the following inaccuracies.**

1 The amounts of fluid held by hospital jugs and cups are not checked if there is no calibration on the side of the jug or cup.
2 The procedure is not explained to the patient, so patient compliance with the procedure is often poor.
3 Amounts are guessed instead of measured.

Share your knowledge

In small groups, discuss the following questions and then feed back your group's ideas to the class.

● Are Fluid Balance Charts used in your country? If not, what is used to record fluid intake and output?
● Have you experienced any problems with Fluid Balance Charts? If so, what did you do about it?

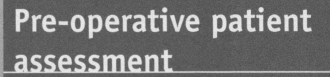

UNIT 8 Pre-operative patient assessment

- Doing pre-operative checks
- Giving pre-operative patient information
- Preparing a patient for surgery
- Allaying anxiety in a patient
- Using Pre-operative Checklists

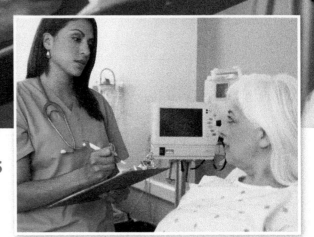

Doing pre-operative checks

1 a **In pairs, discuss the following questions.**

1 What is your experience of pre-operative (pre-op) checks?
2 Why are pre-op procedures important?
3 What problems can occur if a pre-op check is not done accurately?

b *Nancy Clarke, a 58-year-old, is booked for elective bowel surgery. Last week, three polyps were discovered in her colon during a diagnostic colonoscopy – the examination of the bowel through an endoscope. Alexandra, the Ward Nurse, prepares Mrs Clarke for her operation by telling her about the pre-operative routine.*

▶ 8.1 **Listen to the conversation and answer the following questions.**

1 What pre-op hygiene instructions does the nurse give Mrs Clarke?
2 Why isn't she allowed to eat or drink before the operation?
3 Why does she have to wear the stockings?

c ▶ 8.1 **Listen again and complete the following sentences.**

1 Yes. _____I'm_____ _____going_____ _____to_____ look at the operation list when it comes out later today ...
2 Now, _____ get you to take off your nail polish later today ...
3 And _____ also need to shower with this antiseptic wash.
4 _____ my tummy be shaved before the operation?
5 ... for a few days. _____ _____ _____ order you clear fluids for today.
6 That means I _____ be able to eat or drink anything after midnight, _____ I?
7 No, not at all. _____ get you to take a special bowel preparation drink later to clean out your bowel. _____ also need a small enema ...

d In pairs, practise explaining pre-operative preparations and asking questions. Student A, you are a nurse; Student B, you are a pre-operative patient. Swap roles and practise again.

Giving pre-operative patient education

2 **a** In pairs, discuss the following questions.

1 What is your experience of pre-operative patient education?
2 Do you use different strategies when dealing with children or patients from different cultural backgrounds?
3 What are the benefits of pre-operative patient education, both for patients and for the healthcare system?

b Match the medical terms (1–5) to their meanings (a–e).

1 thrombus	a the process of blood clotting
2 anti-embolic	b deep vein thrombosis
3 DVT	c usually refers to a medication which inhibits the formation of thromboses
4 anticoagulant	d solid mass which forms in blood vessels; also called a *blood clot*
5 coagulation	e stops an embolus from forming

c In pairs, read the post-op information sheet and the typical patient questions (1–7). Practise asking and answering the questions. Student A, you are a patient; ask the questions. Student B, you are a nurse; find answers to the questions using the information sheet. Swap roles and practise again.

1 Is this something to do with clots?
2 How do I put the stockings on?
3 Are they different from ordinary stockings?
4 When do I have to start wearing them?
5 I won't have to wear these permanently, I hope?
6 Will I have to walk on my own?
7 How long will I have to have the injections?

Post-operative instructions: mobilisation post-op

There are some important things which will be part of your post-operative recovery. You'll wear anti-embolic stockings, mobilise gradually and be on anticoagulant therapy. These measures are important in order to prevent blood clots (also called DVTs, or Deep Vein Thromboses).

a Anti-embolic stockings
- Graduated compression stockings which provide varying pressure to your lower limbs
- Worn two hours pre-op and post-op until you return to full mobility
- Must be put on smoothly (no bunching of the stocking)

b Early ambulation
- You will be encouraged to get moving again soon after your operation
- Frequent short walks around the ward with assistance if necessary

c Anticoagulant therapy
- Subcutaneous injections of heparin twice a day
- Anticoagulant therapy continues until fully mobile

Preparing a patient for surgery

Research suggests that patients who are physically and psychologically prepared for surgery tend to have better outcomes after surgery.

3 **a** **In pairs, discuss the following questions.**

1 What would you talk to a patient about before surgery?
2 Do you have any experience of working in a surgical ward?
3 What are the challenges of working in a surgical ward?
4 What changes have there been in abdominal surgery in recent years?
5 How are patients prepared for abdominal surgery?

b **Match the medical terms (1–6) to their meanings (a–f).**

1 gallbladder	a drug which blocks pain and other sensations before an operation is performed
2 laparoscope	b safety measure which prevents patients from continually obtaining analgesia by pressing a patient-control button
3 anaesthetic	c patient-controlled analgesia
4 PCA	d surgical instrument which is inserted into the abdomen to visualise the abdominal organs
5 overdose	e abdominal organ which stores bile
6 lock-out time	f taking excess amounts of medication with serious health consequences

c **In pairs, take turns to say a term and ask your partner to define it.**

d ▶ 8.2 **Ms Emma Slade, a nervous 45-year-old, is booked for an elective cholecystectomy (removal of the gallbladder) tomorrow. Listen to Alva, the Ward Nurse, explaining what Emma can expect when she returns to the ward after her operation, and answer the following questions.**

1 How is Emma feeling about her operation?
2 What kind of surgery is she going to have?
3 What is the name of the instrument the surgeon will use to visualise her gallbladder?
4 Why won't she have a large scar after her operation?
5 How long will the mini-drain stay in after the operation?
6 What will the nurses check before she can eat and drink after her operation?
7 When will the nurses remove her urinary catheter?

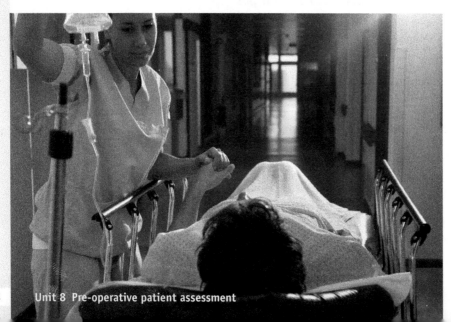

e ▶8.2 **Before Alva talks to Emma about her operation, she makes some notes to help her remember everything she needs to say. Listen again and match Alva's notes (1–8) to her explanations (a–h).**

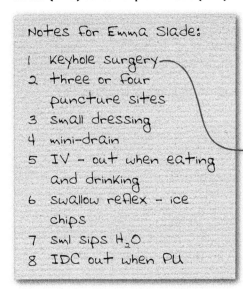

Notes for Emma Slade:

1 keyhole surgery
2 three or four puncture sites
3 small dressing
4 mini-drain
5 IV - out when eating and drinking
6 swallow reflex - ice chips
7 sml sips H₂O
8 IDC out when PU

a   You'll come back with an IV and some fluids running, just until you can eat and drink again.
b   It can be taken out when you're back on the ward and think you can void again – I mean, pass urine.
c   We check that you can swallow again by trying you with a few ice chips.
d   It's a small plastic container attached to some tubing which takes away any excess blood from your wound.
e   ... also called minimally invasive surgery because it's performed with the use of a laparoscope, using small incisions or surgical cuts.
f   These are just small holes made near your navel.
g   As soon as you can manage the ice chips, we'll give you small sips of water.
h   It's just a light covering to keep the area clean until it heals.

Communication focus: allaying anxiety in a patient

4 a **In pairs, discuss the following questions.**

1   What strategies have you used successfully to allay anxiety in a patient?
2   Would you use different strategies for different age groups?
3   What strategies might also be useful for a child?
4   What strategies would you use for a patient who didn't speak English?

b **Complete the following strategies for allaying anxiety in a patient using the words in the box.**

involve ~~rapport~~ normal anxiety reassuring avoid

1   Establish a ___rapport___ with the patient, as this helps to decrease the feeling of depersonalisation and isolation.
2   Use a calm, _____ approach.
3   Explain that anxiety is a _____ reaction.
4   Help identify situations which cause _____ , for example fear of anaesthesia.
5   Try to _____ words which increase anxiety; for example, use *discomfort* rather than *pain*.
6   Try to _____ the patient in decision-making wherever possible, as this decreases the sense of loss of control.

c ▶ 8.3 **Listen to the rest of the conversation between Alva and Emma and answer the following questions.**

1 What concern does Emma have about using the PCA?
2 What safety measure on the machine does Alva explain?
3 What will the nurses check frequently after the operation?
4 How often will Emma use her tri-ball after the operation?
5 What do you think Alva's second post-operative instruction might be?

d **Alva used several strategies to allay anxiety in response to Emma's concerns. Match the concerns (1–5) to the responses (a–e).**

1 Is everything all right? There's nothing wrong, is there?	a No, not much, but I can make a note for the rest of the staff to cover the drain for you so you don't see any of it.
2 I feel silly being so worried. I'm not normally like this.	b No, don't worry. We program the pump so there's a lock-out time.
3 There won't be lots of blood, will there? I can't stand the sight of blood.	c No, not at all, everything's fine.
4 What about pain? I'm worried that I'll be in a lot of pain.	d That's OK, Emma. It's quite normal to feel a bit apprehensive.
5 But what if I keep pushing the button? Won't I give myself an overdose?	e You'll have a PCA machine to use for any discomfort after the operation. That's what I wanted to show you ...

e **In pairs, discuss which strategies Alva used when talking to Emma. Can you think of any other strategies?**

f *Nashida Hussein, a 24-year-old university student, has been admitted for an elective appendicectomy. She is very anxious about the operation.*

In pairs, practise allaying patient anxiety. Student A, you are Nashida; read the questions on page 90 and be ready to ask the nurse for the information you need. Student B, you are the nurse; read the patient information sheet on page 89 and be ready to answer Nashida's questions. Remember to use strategies to allay anxiety. Swap roles and practise again.

Share your knowledge

In small groups, discuss the following questions and then feed back your group's ideas to the class.

- Is patient education an important nursing focus in your country?
- Have you been involved in patient education in your country? If so, what did you find challenging about delivering patient education? What did you find rewarding?

Medical focus: blood circulation

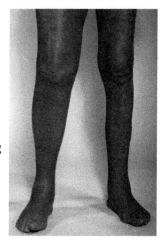

5 **a** In pairs, look at the picture and discuss the following questions.

1 What does the picture illustrate?
2 Do you have experience of caring for patients with this medical condition?

b ▶8.4 Mr Vitellis, a 56-year-old teacher, has recently been hospitalised for orthopaedic surgery following a skiing accident. Listen to a conversation between Mr Vitellis and Nasreen, the Ward Nurse, and mark the following statements True (T) or False (F).

1 Mr Vitellis underwent an orthopaedic operation which took several hours.
2 He showed no signs of having a blood clot after his operation.
3 His condition is being treated with anticoagulant medication.
4 He had both anti-embolic stockings removed after the operation.
5 He has developed a pulmonary embolism.
6 He is free from pain and leaving the hospital today.

c Match the medical terms (1–5) to their meanings (a–e).

1 venodilation	a the condition which is caused when a blood clot blocks blood flow
2 embolus	b the pooling of blood in the veins
3 embolism	c stretching or widening of a vein
4 venous stasis	d a blood clot which breaks off and moves freely along a blood vessel

d Underline the stressed syllable in words 1–4.

e Label the following diagram using the words in the box.

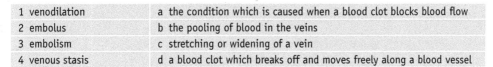

embolism   DVT   normal blood flow   embolus

1 _____   2 _____   3 _____   4 _____

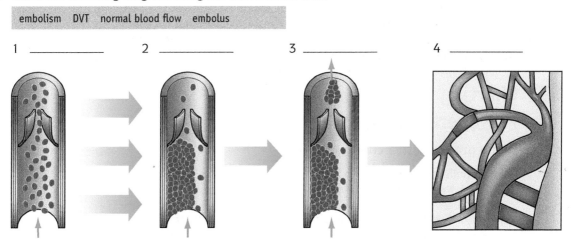

f ▶8.4 Put the following stages of DVT in the correct order. Listen again and check your answers to this and Exercise 5e.

☐ Formation of an embolus
☐ Venous stasis caused by immobility
☐ Blood becomes stickier and coagulates more easily
☐ Venodilation causes small tears in the inner walls of the veins
☐ An embolus blocks blood flow

g Complete the following explanations of the medication used to treat DVT, using the words in the box.

> warfarin   pulmonary embolism   filter   ~~anticoagulant~~
> INR   DVTs   subcutaneous   heparin   lifelong   dose

1 When a DVT forms in a patient's leg, they are given _anticoagulant_ medication.
2 Most patients start treatment with _____ whilst in hospital.
3 Heparin, an anticoagulant medication, is usually given as a _____ injection – that is, under the skin.
4 As well as heparin injections, patients start on the oral anticoagulant called
   _____ .
5 Patients will probably have to take the warfarin tablets for three to six months after leaving hospital unless they've had problems with _____ or _____ in the past. In these cases, they may require _____ warfarin therapy.
6 Warfarin therapy often requires frequent _____ adjustment and regular monitoring of the _____ through a blood test.
7 If anticoagulant therapy is not effective or contra-indicated, the doctor may talk to patients about having an IVC _____ implanted.

h *Mrs Heather Perry is taking the oral contraceptive pill and has recently returned from a long-haul flight. Mrs Perry has two of the risk factors for getting DVTs: hormone therapy, such as the oral contraceptive pill, and long periods of sitting immobile. She has been admitted to hospital with a suspected DVT in her right calf and is very concerned about her condition.*

In pairs, practise explaining how DVTs form, including some of the risk factors, and the likely treatment plan. Student A, you are the nurse; Student B, you are Heather Perry. Remember to use strategies to allay anxiety in a patient. Swap roles and practise again.

Charting and documentation: Pre-operative Checklist

Doing pre-operative checks

Before a patient is transferred to the Operating Theatres, all relevant charts and X-rays are gathered before a final ward check is made.

6 a In pairs, look at the chart on page 90 and discuss the following questions.

1 When is this chart used?
2 Are you familiar with this type of chart?

b ▶ 8.5 Viki, the Ward Nurse, is checking Belinda Mainwaring for surgery. Listen to the conversation and complete the blue shaded parts of the Pre-operative Checklist. Tick in the appropriate boxes marked YES or NO or N/A (Not Applicable).

c *Patients pass from the care of one person to another several times on the way to surgery, and pre-operative information is checked by various staff members. Belinda is in the Operating Theatre holding area before she is taken in to have her operation performed.*

▶ 8.6 **Wendy, the Theatre Nurse, checks the patient details and details relating to the operation. She uses the green shaded area in the column marked O/T (Operating Theatre). Listen to the conversation and tick the sections of the Checklist on page 90 that Wendy double-checks.**

d ▶ 8.6 **Listen again and put the following extracts in the correct order.**

☐ I know you've already answered many of these questions, but we like to double-check everything.

☐ I'll sign the Checklist, and you've already got a theatre cap to cover your hair.

☐ I'll have a quick look at your identification bracelets if I may?

☐ Can you tell me your full name, please?

☐ Is this your signature on the consent form?

☐ Did you sign a consent form for the operation?

☒ I'm going to check you in today.

☐ Have you had a pre-med?

☐ I'm just going to go through this Checklist again.

☐ Can you tell me what operation you're having today?

e **In pairs, practise going through the Pre-operative Checklist. Student A, you are the Theatre Nurse; Student B, you are the patient. Swap roles and practise again.**

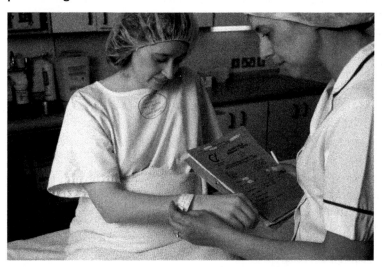

Share your knowledge

In small groups, discuss the following questions and then feed back your group's ideas to the class.

1 What pre-operative procedures are you familiar with?
2 Are procedures different in your country?
3 What are the benefits of having several checks before the patient has an operation?

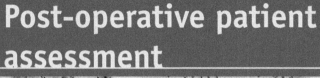

UNIT 9 Post-operative patient assessment

- Giving a post-operative handover
- Checking a post-operative patient on the ward
- Explaining post-operative pain management
- Dealing with aggressive behaviour
- Using pain assessment tools

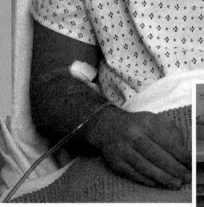

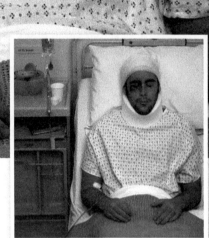

Giving a post-operative handover

1 a In pairs, discuss the following questions.

1 What is your experience of post-op handovers?
2 What information and documentation needs to be passed on to the Ward Nurse during the post-op handover?
3 What sort of things does the Ward Nurse crosscheck when a patient comes back from an operation?
4 How is a post-op handover different from a change-of-shift handover?
5 Why is it important to check the patient regularly after an operation?

b *Roli Davidson, a 28-year-old who has had surgery following a road traffic accident (RTA), comes back to the ward. Hazel, the Recovery Nurse, hands Roli over to Georgia, the Ward Nurse. Georgia conducts an initial return-to-ward check and starts Roli on post-op observations.*

▶ **9.1 Listen to the conversation and answer the following questions.**

1 What operation has Roli just had?
2 Why did the Recovery Nurses monitor Roli carefully after his operation?
3 Why will Roli continue to receive IV fluids on the ward?
4 Is Roli's redivac draining properly?
5 How did the surgeon close Roli's wound?
6 Will the ward nurses have to re-dress Roli's wound this evening?
7 Has Roli already had some pain relief?
8 Why did the Recovery Nurse give Roli an extra blanket?

c Match the abbreviations (1–6) to their meanings (a–f).

1 RTA	a Glasgow Coma Scale; records the conscious state of a patient
2 GCS	b Non-Adhesive Dressing
3 neuro obs.	c measure of the amount of oxygen which is loaded or saturated into the red blood cells as they pass through the lungs
4 oxygen sats / SaO$_2$	d from the Latin *pro re nata*: take whenever required
5 NAD	e observations which assess neurological function and include a GCS assessment
6 prn	f road traffic accident

d ▶9.1 **Listen again and fill in the missing information on Roli Davidson's Operation Report using the words and figures in the box.**

> oral redivac intact 36° dextrose 97 13/15
> patent 72 clips NAD 75 ~~RTA~~

Name of patient	Roli Davidson
Operation performed	Splenectomy post (1) _____RTA_____
GCS before leaving Recovery	(2) _____
Observations	T (3) _____ P (4) _____ BP 112/64
	SaO$_2$ (5) _____ % on 3L/min
IV therapy	1L 5% (6) _____
Drains	Redivac x 1 (7) _____ and draining small amounts
Wound closure	(8) _____ x 6
Wound	Covered with (9) _____
Analgesia	Pethidine (10) _____ mg IM 3° for 3 days then
	(11) _____ analgesia
Post-op instructions	Remove (12) _____ when draining < 20ml/day
	Leave dressing (13) _____ until surgeon's review

e In pairs, practise handing over a post-operative patient. Student A, you are a Recovery Nurse; Student B, you are a Ward Nurse. Use the role card on page 91. Swap roles and practise again.

Checking a post-operative patient on the ward

2 a ▶9.2 **Listen to Georgia talking to Roli and answer the following questions.**

1 Is Roli's temperature back to normal?
2 What is the nurse going to get him for his sore throat?
3 Does he feel like eating after his operation?
4 Is he pain free at the moment?
5 Has he been up to the toilet to pass urine?
6 How can he call the nurse if he needs her?

b ▶9.2 **Listen again and match the feelings (1–8) to their explanations (a–h).**

1 I'm still feeling cold. Is that normal?
2 I'm awake now, but I still feel a bit groggy.
3 My throat feels really sore. It's hard to swallow.
4 I feel like I'd be sick if I ate anything.
5 I'm in bad pain, and everything hurts.
6 I feel like I can't move because it's going to be painful.
7 I feel as if I want to go to the toilet all the time.
8 I feel dizzy, too. It's like I'm going to fall out of bed.

a That's OK. It takes a little while to be orientated again after an anaesthetic.
b That's quite normal. Patients who've had abdominal surgery are often in quite a bit of discomfort.
c Yeah, it's OK. It's called hypothermia. It happens sometimes if the operation takes a long time.
d It's quite common to avoid any movement which might cause discomfort, but it's important that I help you to move around and change position.
e That's because you've had an anaesthetic.
f It's quite usual to have that sensation, even though you've got a catheter in your bladder.
g Nausea is sometimes a reaction to post-operative pain.
h Don't worry, that's normal. It's just caused by the tube they put down your throat during surgery.

c In pairs, practise expressing feelings and explaining the cause. Student A, you are Georgia; Student B, you are Roli. Use Exercise 2b and your own ideas. Swap roles and practise again.

Explaining post-operative pain management

3 **a** *Paul Vargas was the victim of an assault and sustained a fractured zygoma (broken cheekbone) and multiple lacerations (cuts) to his arms and chest. After surgery he is in pain and requires careful pain management.*

▶ **9.3 Listen to a conversation between Paul and Patricia, the Ward Nurse, and answer the following questions.**

1   How does Paul rate his pain?
2   Why has he been ordered paracetamol?
3   What does the nurse do to help him sleep?

b Paul describes his pain to Patricia. Complete the following extracts using the words in the box. Can you think of any other ways to describe pain?

hurts   throbbing   hurt   knife   stinging

1   My arms _____ where the cuts are.
2   I've got a _____ headache.
3   My right cheek _____ when I touch it.
4   It's a _____ pain in the shallow cuts.
5   This cut in my chest is quite deep, and the pain's like a _____ .

c ▶ **9.3 Listen again and match Patricia's questions (1–8) to Paul's answers (a–h).**

1 How are you feeling now?
2 Can you tell me where the pain is?
3 Can you tell me if the pain is the same all over or different?
4 What about the pain in your arms and chest?
5 When's the pain worse, Paul?
6 What's the pain like now you are at rest?
7 And when you move a bit?
8 Is there anything else which relieves the pain?

a Yeah. My head, my cheek ... um, the broken cheek, I mean ...
b It's a stinging pain in the shallow cuts, but this cut in my chest is quite deep, and the pain's like a knife.
c Oh, not too good. Everything hurts.
d It gets worse. Seven, at least.
e One of the nurses gave me a heat pack for my chest, and that helped.
f I've got a throbbing headache, and my right cheek hurts when I touch it.
g It's worse when I turn over or move.
h It's around six.

d   In pairs, practise rating pain and explaining how to manage pain. Student A, you are a patient in severe pain after a car accident and have multiple fractures and lacerations. Student B, you are the Ward Nurse; ask the patient to rate the pain level on the pain scale and explain to them how to manage the pain. Swap roles and practise again.

Share your knowledge

1   What other words can describe pain?
2   What kind of pain could each of these words describe?
    aching   cramping   crushing   throbbing   radiating
3   What are some examples of *pain behaviours* that chronic pain sufferers might exhibit?
4   Why might chronic pain sufferers exhibit these behaviours?
5   Have you had experience of caring for a patient with chronic pain? Did you encounter any difficulties with his/her pain management?

Dealing with aggressive behaviour

The hospital environment is often stressful for relatives and friends of patients, especially when they witness a loved one in pain. Sometimes, tense situations can develop into aggressive behaviour towards staff members.

4 **a In pairs, discuss the following questions.**
- Have you had any experience of dealing with aggressive or violent individuals in a healthcare environment?
- What strategies can you use to calm the situation?

b ▶9.4 Listen to a conversation between Patricia and Bev, another Ward Nurse, and answer the following questions.
1 Why are the nurses staying at the Nurses' Station?
2 Why is Paul's visitor, Mr Fellows, angry?
3 How do the nurses react to him?
4 What does the nurse ask him to do so she can understand him?
5 How does the nurse reassure him about Paul?

c *Many hospitals have Aggressive Behaviour Management (ABM) protocols which are followed when dealing with patients or visitors.*

Complete the staff information sheet on the right using the words in the box.

> solution listen defuse speak ~~observe~~ empathise
> alternative rephrase

d In pairs, read the audioscript on page 106 and find examples of the ABM techniques that the nurses used with Mr Fellows.

e *Mrs Charmaine Berry has arrived at Neurology after a long wait in A&E. She is complaining of a severe migraine which she has rated as an 8 on the pain scale, despite receiving analgesia. The doctor has been paged but, unfortunately, has been delayed by an emergency. Mr Berry is becoming visibly agitated by his wife's pain and has approached a nurse on the ward to demand immediate attention for his wife.*

In pairs, practise defusing a tense situation. Student A, you are the nurse; Student B, you are Mr Berry. Swap roles and practise again.

Aggressive Behaviour Management (ABM) Techniques

All staff are to follow these guidelines to avoid the escalation of violence in the workplace. Aggressive behaviour towards staff will not be tolerated and will be dealt with by security if necessary.

ABM Guidelines

- (1) ___Observe___ a potentially aggressive situation and attempt to (2) _____ it before things get out of hand.
- (3) _____ calmly to what the patient or visitor is trying to tell you.
- (4) _____ in a quiet but firm tone in order to calm the situation.
- (5) _____ what the patient or visitor tells you to demonstrate your understanding.
- (6) _____ by indicating that you can understand why they are upset.
- Offer a (7) _____ to the problem or an (8) _____ if a solution is not possible.

Share your knowledge

In small groups, discuss the following questions and then feed back your group's ideas to the class.
1 Is aggressive or violent behaviour towards nursing staff a problem in your country?
2 What do you think are the reasons behind this type of behaviour?
3 What initiatives would you like to see taken to address this serious issue?

Medical focus: pain receptors

Post-operative pain is experienced at different levels, depending on the extent of surgical trauma. The type of surgery, the patient's preparation for surgery and the patient's previous experience of surgery also play a part in pain tolerance.

5 **a** **Read the patient information leaflet and answer the following questions.**

1 Where does cutaneous pain originate from?
2 What is the pain which originates in body organs called?
3 What are the two types of pain fibre called?
4 What is the difference between fast and slow pain?
5 What is a common term for analgesia?

Post-operative pain management

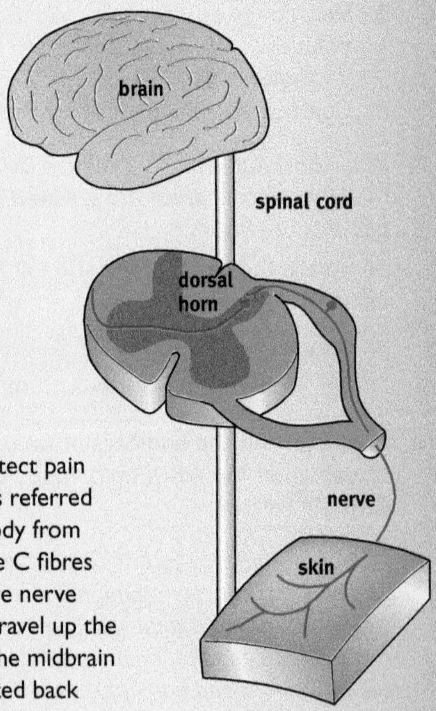

The two types of pain which you may experience in the post-operative setting are called cutaneous and visceral pain. After a surgical incision, pain-causing substances are released. These chemical substances cause cutaneous nociceptors, or free nerve endings, to detect the injury to the skin. This is known as 'fast pain' and is sharp or acute. It is also localised pain, meaning it is only felt in the area of the injury. Nociceptors transmit impulses using afferent nerves (nerves which carry impulses towards the central nervous system) through Type A-delta fibres. The fast, sharp pain impulses travel via peripheral nerves to the dorsal horn at the back of the spinal cord. Here they synapse, or connect, with the second type of fibres, Type C fibres. Type C fibres detect visceral pain. Visceral nociceptors are found in all the organs of the body and detect pain impulses as slow, aching pain. Slow pain is also described as referred pain – that is, pain which is felt in a different part of the body from the original injury. In the dorsal horn, Type A-delta and Type C fibres synapse with dendrites in the spinal cord (extensions of the nerve cell body that receive signals from other nerve cells) and travel up the spine as neurons or nerve impulses. They then ascend to the midbrain where the nerve impulses are processed and are transmitted back to the body as a pain signal. The type of pain, cutaneous or visceral, determines the choice of analgesia, or pain relief, that you will be given for your post-operative pain.

Diagram labels: brain, spinal cord, dorsal horn, nerve, skin

b **Match the medical terms (1–6) to their meanings (a–f).**

1 nociceptor	a relating to the skin
2 cutaneous	b a cut into the skin; often refers to a surgical cut
3 visceral	c a pain which is felt in a part of the body away from the injury site
4 incision	d referring to the internal organs of the body
5 localised pain	e a receptor which detects painful stimuli
6 referred pain	f pain which is felt around the site of an injury

c **Underline the stressed syllable in words 1–6.**

d ▶9.5 **Listen to Sonia, the hospital Pharmacist, talking about post-operative analgesia. Match the medical terms (1–9) to their meanings (a–i).**

1 pain threshold	a medication which is given in between doses where more pain relief is needed
2 pain tolerance	b a medication which brings down a high temperature
3 NSAIDs	c the most pain which a person can put up with
4 opioids	d opiate proteins with pain-relieving properties which occur naturally in the brain
5 endorphins	e treatment which combines several types of pain management
6 anti-pyretic	f level of stimulation required before pain felt
7 background drug	g drugs which produce a morphine-like effect
8 multimodal	h non-steroid anti-inflammatory drugs; also called *non-steroidals*
9 breakthrough dose	i a drug used to support the main analgesic; often used to reduce the amount needed of opioid medication

e ▶9.5 **Listen again and complete the following notes using the words in the box.**

multimodal   threshold   non-steroidals   background   scale   tolerance
~~acute~~   morphine-like

Post-operative pain is (1) _____acute_____ pain
Pain (2) _____ - point at which everyone experiences something as painful
Pain (3) _____ - subjective, different experience for each patient
Pain (4) _____ - used to assess individual pain level
Surgical incision causes localised pain - (5) _____ , anti-inflammatory drugs most effective
Visceral pain causes referred pain - opioids or (6) _____ drugs most effective
Drugs such as paracetamol are added as (7) _____ drugs to reduce amount of opioids needed
(8) _____ treatment - when different kinds of treatment are used at the same time

f **In groups of three, look at the audioscript on page 106. Student A, make notes on the use of opioids; Student B, make notes on the use of non-steroidals; Student C, make notes on the use of paracetamol. Using only your notes, take it in turns to explain your topic. Be prepared to answer questions from the group.**

Share your knowledge

In small groups, discuss the following questions and then feed back your group's ideas to the class.

1 What can happen if pain remains untreated or is not dealt with sympathetically?
2 Do you think pain is experienced differently in different cultures?
3 Do you have any experience of different pain responses because of cultural background? If so, how did you help your patient deal with his/her pain?

Charting and documentation: pain assessment

6 **a** **In pairs, look at the chart on page 91 and answer the following questions.**

    1 What is this chart for?

    2 Are you familiar with this type of chart?

    3 What is the scale that uses diagrams of different facial expressions called?

    4 What other types of rating scale are found on this chart?

    5 Why do you think these types of assessment chart are important?

b *Six-year-old Anton had a tonsillectomy yesterday. The Ward Nurse, Sharon, talks to him and his mother, Sarah, about pain relief. Sharon is wearing a large badge with her name on and a picture of a friendly cartoon character.*

▶ **9.6 Sharon explains the Wong–Baker faces to Anton and Sarah. Listen to the conversation and answer the following questions.**

    1 What does Anton get as a reward after his medication?

    2 Which face does he point to?

    3 What does the nurse get him to play with?

c ▶ **9.6 Listen again and match the description of the faces in the chart (1–6) to Sharon's explanations (a–f).**

1 Face number 1: no pain	a He's got quite a lot of pain. It hurts when he moves about.
2 Face number 2: mild pain which can be ignored	b Can you see that he looks really unhappy? He's got a frown on his face, and he can't concentrate on anything.
3 Face number 3: moderate pain which interferes with tasks	c This poor guy's crying and can't even get out of bed because it hurts so much. It's the worst pain he's ever felt.
4 Face number 4: moderate pain which interferes with concentration	d Can you see he's smiling? He feels great. Nothing hurts.
5 Face number 5: severe pain which interferes with basic needs	e And the next little fellow's feeling worse. The pain's very bad now. He's feeling very bad.
6 Face number 6: worst pain possible, bed rest required	f The next face feels pretty good, but it hurts a little bit. He can put up with it.

d **Sharon and Sarah use question tags when they speak to Anton. Complete the following sentences using the question tags in the box. Why do you think they use question tags?**

> isn't he?   doesn't it?   shall we?   don't you?   is he?

    1 I think Anton likes the stickers I give him after his medicine even better,

       _____

    2 He's starting to look a bit sad, _____

    3 He's not very happy at all, _____

    4 Playing games always takes your mind off feeling uncomfortable,

       _____

    5 We'll let mum go and have a cup of coffee, _____

e In pairs, look at the strategies for dealing with a child in pain (1–7). Have you used any of these before?

1   Try to form a relationship with the child by using inclusive language.
2   Wear a name badge with your first name and introduce yourself to the child.
3   Use a soothing, reassuring voice.
4   Use appropriate language for any explanations.
5   Use humour to relax an otherwise tense situation.
6   Reassure the child that you will help them to feel better and reduce their pain.
7   Use therapeutic games to take the child's attention off the pain.

f Match the sentences from the conversation (a–g) to a strategy in Exercise 6e (1–7).

a   It's Sharon. She's got that name badge on that you like. 2
b   I think Anton likes the stickers I give him after his medicine even better, don't you?
c   Mm, still hurts to talk, doesn't it, Anton?
d   I'm going to show you my sad and happy faces. They're very useful for kids who can't talk because they've got a sore throat.
e   Now, Anton, can you help me by pointing to the face which is showing how you feel right now?
f   I'm going to get you some medicine to help your sore throat, but I want you to tell me first how much it hurts.
g   Playing games always takes your mind off feeling uncomfortable, doesn't it?

g In pairs, discuss the following questions.

•   What other strategies have you used successfully to distract a child from post-operative pain?
•   Which strategies have not been successful?
•   Have you ever had any difficulties pacifying a child in pain?

h *Lucas, a 7-year-old, has had a repair of an inguinal hernia this morning. His father, Anthony, has asked for some pain relief for his son.*

In pairs, practise explaining and using the Wong–Baker faces chart. Student A, you are a Ward Nurse; Student B, you are Lucas. Swap roles and practise again.

Share your knowledge

In small groups, discuss the following questions and then feed back your group's ideas to the class.

1   Which other groups of people might the Wong–Baker faces chart be useful for?
2   How might you adapt the Wong–Baker faces chart for a young visually impaired patient?
3   How might the Wong–Baker faces chart be adapted to assess other problems patients may have?

UNIT 10 | Discharge planning

- Attending the ward team meeting
- Telephone skills: referring a patient
- Explaining the effects of a stroke
- Using patient discharge planning forms

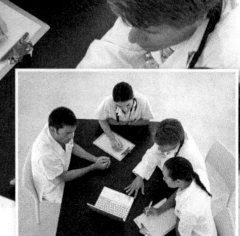

Attending the ward team meeting

Most hospital wards have a weekly team meeting to discuss the progress of certain patients. The members of the team involved in the patient's care meet to talk about care after discharge from hospital, and plan any assistance which may be needed.

1 a In pairs, discuss the following questions.

1 Why is collaboration between healthcare professionals important?
2 What are some of the difficulties that might occur during team meetings?
3 What is your experience of ward team meetings?

b *Andrea, a Rehab Ward Sister, is chairing a team meeting to discuss Lidia, an 80-year-old patient who has recently suffered a stroke. After a period of rehabilitation in hospital she is now ready for discharge.*

▶10.1 **Listen to the meeting and mark the following statements True (T) or False (F).**

1 Lidia has always been very independent.
2 Her daughters found her unconscious.
3 She had been drinking and was slurring her speech.
4 She had a stroke while they were visiting her.
5 She will need help with her ADLs.
6 The Occupational Therapist team have done a home assessment.
7 She still has difficulty with her speech.

c ▶10.1 **Listen again and answer the following questions.**

1 How long has Lidia been in hospital?
2 What is her main goal?
3 What day is the home assessment booked for?
4 What special arrangements were made regarding her food?
5 Where is she going to stay when she first gets out of hospital?
6 When is her expected date of discharge?

d Match the phrases (1–6) to the functions in a meeting (a–c).

1 Let's start with ... 2 The purpose of this meeting is ... 3 William, do you want to kick off? 4 I agree with both of you. 5 Yes, I'm a bit worried about that as well. 6 Tina, what about ...	a Managing the meeting b Including/inviting other people in/into the discussion c Agreeing with colleagues

e Mr Eddie Trumpett, a 55-year-old stroke victim, is going home to his wife and two teenage children. In groups of four, practise taking part in a team meeting. Student A, you are a Nurse; Student B, you are a Speech and Language Therapist; Student C, you are a Physiotherapist; Student D, you are a Doctor. Remember to use the phrases from Exercise 1d.

Telephone skills: referring a patient

2 a Ward staff often need to make telephone referrals to allied health departments or services. In pairs, look at the telephone referral form below and discuss the following questions.

1 Who referred Lidia to the District Nursing Service?
2 Where was she referred from?
3 Who is her next of kin?

TELEPHONE REFERRAL FORM	
Service referred to	District Nursing Service
Name of patient	Lidia (1) ___Vassily___
Address	24 Spring Lane, Exeter
Entry to home (circle)	Digital Code / (Key) If by key, name of carer with spare key: (2) _____
Phone number	(3) _____
GP	Dr Serena (4) _____
Referred by	Andrea Dubois (RN)
Place of referral	Alexandra Hospital
Diagnosis	Stroke, mod. left-sided weakness, difficulty swallowing
Assistance with ADLs (circle)	(5) bathing mobility nutrition
Diet (circle)	(6) normal soft diabetic Other requirements (cultural/religious)
Delivery of meals (circle)	(7) Yes/No
Home assessment booked (circle)	(8) Yes/No If Yes, date booked: (9) _____
Aids / Equipment (circle if need to be ordered)	walking frame shower chair oxygen nebuliser
Next of kin	Larissa (daughter)
Phone number:	01265 781 992

b ▶10.2 Andrea, the Ward Nurse, rings Nadine, the District Nurse, to discuss Lidia's referral to the District Nursing Service. Listen to the conversation and complete the sections of the referral form marked 1–9.

c Speaking on the telephone to fluent speakers is often particularly difficult when under pressure. In pairs, discuss the following questions.

1 Have you had difficulties with telephone communication?
2 What types of situation have you found challenging?
3 Which of the following strategies for effective telephone communication have you used?

> **Strategies for effective telephone communication**
>
> ♦ Ask the fluent speaker to slow down as soon as you have difficulty understanding.
>
> ♦ Don't wait to ask the speaker to slow down until you are really lost.
>
> ♦ When you are taking down important details, repeat the information back so that you are sure you have understood.
>
> ♦ Do not be embarrassed to ask more than once if you are still not sure.

d ▶ 10.2 Listen to the telephone conversation again and tick the sentences you hear. You may hear both sentences in each pair.

1 a ☐ I'm sorry. What was your name again, please?
  b ☐ Sorry, what was your name?
2 a ☐ Could you please spell that for me?
  b ☐ Can you spell it?
3 a ☐ Can you say that again, please?
  b ☐ Could you please repeat that? I didn't catch the last numbers.
4 a ☐ Sorry, I didn't catch that.
  b ☐ Would you mind speaking a little slower, please? I'm having trouble following you.

e In pairs, practise making a referral for district nursing services. Student A, you are a Ward Nurse; Student B, you are a District Nurse. Use the referral form on page 79 and Mr Vogel's notes on page 91. Remember to use effective telephone strategies. Swap roles and practise again.

f *Nurses often have to handle patient enquiries over the phone. It is important to assist the caller as much as possible whilst remembering to respect patient confidentiality at all times. Mr Bouchard had a fall at home and has been in hospital for four weeks after suffering a stroke. His daughter, Gillian, phones the Ward Nurse, Simon, for some advice.*

▶ 10.3 Listen to the conversation and answer the following questions.

1 What can happen to a person's emotional state after a stroke?
2 Who will Simon ask to call Gillian?
3 Why can't Simon discuss Mr Bouchard's progress with Gillian?
4 Who does he suggest Gillian speak to and why?

g In pairs, discuss the following concerns that patients have when they call a hospital. Have you dealt with callers who had any of these concerns?

1 Callers sometimes feel they are a nuisance.
2 Callers do not know the title or rank of the person they are speaking to.
3 Callers are concerned they will be cut off or not directed to the correct department.
4 Callers worry that they will not be taken seriously.
5 Callers worry that their concern will not be dealt with efficiently.
6 Callers don't know what information they can request and what is confidential.

h ▶10.3 Listen again and match the concerns in Exercise 2g (1–6) to what Simon says to address the concern (a–f).

a I'll make a note in Mr Bouchard's notes and pass the message on to his Key Worker. _5_
b I can understand why you're concerned.
c I'm afraid I can't talk to you about your father's results because of confidentiality.
d I'm a Staff Nurse on this ward.
e Not at all. I'm happy to help you if I can.
f I'll give you his direct number in case I can't put you through.

i In pairs, practise Gillian and Simon's telephone call using the following prompts. Swap roles and practise again.

G: Ask to speak to nurse
S: Confirm that you are looking after patient
G: Concerned about father's moods
S: Express understanding / pass information to Key Worker
G: Ask for test results
S: Decline / patient confidentiality / details of Discharge Planning Nurse

Share your knowledge

In small groups, discuss the following questions and then feed back your group's ideas to the class.

1 Do you have the same privacy rules regarding patient information in your country?
2 How else are patient records kept confidential?

Medical Focus: cerebrovascular accidents

The extent of the damage caused during a cerebrovascular accident (CVA), or stroke, depends on the area of the brain which is affected.

3 a In pairs, discuss the following questions.

1 What damage is caused to the body by CVA, or stroke?
2 What are some of the long-term problems of stroke?
3 Have you had experience of nursing a patient who has suffered a stroke?

b Match the medical terms (1–7) to their meanings (a–g).

1 hemisphere	a type of stroke caused when a thrombus blocks the carotid artery, resulting in ischaemia and tissue necrosis; the most common type of stroke
2 carotid artery	b area underneath the brain where the cerebral arteries are linked
3 Circle of Willis	c cerebrovascular accident, or stroke; *cerebro* means brain
4 ischaemia	d type of stroke caused when a blood vessel bursts causing blood to leak into the brain; causes around one fifth of strokes
5 CVA	e inadequate blood supply caused by a blockage in the blood vessel; *isch* means deficiency or lack of
6 ischaemic stroke	f either of the two arteries which supply blood to the brain
7 haemorrhagic stroke	g one of the two regions of the brain; *hemi* means half

c Underline the stressed syllable in words 1–7.

d Complete the following text describing an ischaemic stroke using the words and phrases in the box.

> branch out   oxygenated   obstruct   ~~80%~~   haemorrhagic   deprived of   cerebral   hemispheres

Ischaemic stroke is the most commonly occurring stroke: (1) _____80%_____ of all strokes.
(2) _____ stroke is less common: 20% of all strokes.

Regions of the brain: the brain is divided into two (3) _____ , or parts.

The Circle of Willis allows blood to (4) _____ and reach the entire brain.

The left and right carotid arteries supply (5) _____ blood to the brain.

Ischaemia results from a blockage in a (6) _____ blood vessel and causes the brain to be (7) _____ oxygen and important nutrients.

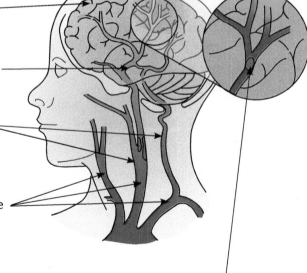

Thrombi which lodge in any of the blood vessels of the brain may (8) _____ blood flow.

Explaining the effects of a stroke

4 a ▶10.4 **Eric Sloane, a 76-year-old retired railway worker, has just suffered a stroke. Katherine, the Ward Nurse, talks to his son and daughter about what happens in ischaemic stroke. Listen to the conversation and mark the following statements True (T) or False (F).**

1 A left CVA ischaemia causes tissue death on the left side of the brain but affects the right side of the body.
2 Mr Sloane has difficulty swallowing because of weakness around the mouth.
3 He is very happy and laughs a lot.
4 A left CVA can cause speech problems.
5 It is important to be patient when you talk to someone who has had a stroke, because they can't hear properly.

b **Match the medical terms (1−8) to their meanings (a−h).**

1 hemiparesis	a motor speech impairment which affects the ability to form words clearly
2 hemiplegia	b difficulty swallowing food or fluids
3 hemianopia	c inappropriate emotional responses, for example laughing when the intention is to cry
4 aphasia	d difficulty expressing what you are thinking
5 dysphasia	e weakness on one side of the body
6 dysphagia	f paralysis on one side of the body
7 dysarthria	g defective vision on one half of the body leads to neglect of one side of the body
8 emotional lability	h inability to communicate

c **Underline the stressed syllable in words 1−8.**

d **In pairs, practise explaining the effects of a stroke. Student A, use the Patient Profile on page 91; Student B, use the Patient Profile on page 93. Read the text on Right CVA below to help you. Be prepared to answer any questions your partner has. Swap roles and practise again.**

RIGHT CVA

The causes of right CVA are the same as for left CVA. Tissue death on the right side of the brain results in damage to functions on the left side of the body. It may cause left hemiparesis, or left-sided weakness, and in more serious cases left hemiplegia – left-sided paralysis. A person with right CVA can also have dysphagia – difficulty swallowing – or dysarthria – difficulty articulating or pronouncing words. Damage to the right side of the brain causes vision problems instead of speech and language problems caused by damage to the left side. Patients with a right CVA may have visual problems like hemianopia, or defective vision, on the right side of the body, making it difficult for them to judge space and distance. They may also neglect the weaker side of the body and ignore objects which are on their left side, meaning that they can fall quite easily. This can be dangerous, especially as people with right CVA tend to behave in an impulsive way, as they are not aware of the extent of the injury to the brain. Short-term memory loss is also a problem.

Charting and documentation: Katz ADL Index

5 **a** **In pairs, look at the chart and answer the following questions.**

1 What is this chart used for?
2 What sort of patient would this chart be useful for?
3 What type of patient might score six?
4 What type of patient might score one?

| U/N: 478261 | Surname: _____ | Given names: _____ | DOB: 12.01.1930 |

ACTIVITIES POINTS (1 OR 0)	INDEPENDENCE (1 POINT) NO supervision, direction or personal assistance	DEPENDENCE (0 POINTS) WITH (f) _____ , direction, personal assistance or total care
BATHING POINTS: ____	(1 POINT) Bathes self completely or needs help in bathing only a single part of the body such as the back, genital area or disabled extremity.	(0 POINTS) Needs help with bathing more than one part of the body, getting in or out of the tub or shower. Requires total bathing.
DRESSING POINTS: ____	(1 POINT) Gets clothes from closets and drawers and puts on clothes and outer garments complete with (a) _____ . May have help tying shoes.	(0 POINTS) Needs help with dressing self or needs to be completely dressed.
TOILETING POINTS: ____	(1 POINT) Goes to toilet, gets on and off toilet, arranges clothes, cleans genital area without help.	(0 POINTS) Needs help to transfer to the toilet, cleaning self, or uses bedpan or (g) _____ .
TRANSFERRING POINTS: ____	(1 POINT) Moves in and out of bed or chair unassisted. (b) _____ are acceptable.	(0 POINTS) Needs help in moving from bed to chair or requires a complete (h) _____ .
FEEDING POINTS: ____	(1 POINT) Gets food from plate into mouth without help. Preparation of food may be done by another person.	(0 POINTS) Needs partial or total help with feeding or requires (i) _____ feeding.
CONTINENCE POINTS: ____	(1 POINT) (c) _____ : exercises complete self-control over (d) _____ and (e) _____ .	(0 POINTS) Is partially or totally (j) _____ of bowel or bladder.
TOTAL POINTS ____	6 = HIGH patient independent 0 = LOW patient very dependent	

b **Match the terms (1–10) to their meanings (a–j).**

1 fasteners	a the act of passing faeces
2 mechanical transferring aids	b devices which join two pieces of clothing together; for example, buttons
3 parenteral	c a chair which contains a bedpan under the seat
4 continent	d watching a patient to ensure an action is performed safely
5 transfer	e administered in any other form but orally, for example by injection or through a feeding tube
6 commode	f not having control of bladder or bowel
7 supervision	g to move from one place to another, for example from bed to chair
8 defecation	h the act of passing urine; also called *micturition*
9 incontinent	i having control of bladder and bowel
10 urination	j mechanical devices used to transfer disabled patients; for example, hoists or sit-to-stand lifters

c **Complete the gaps in the Katz Index in Exercise 5a (a–j) using the terms from Exercise 4b.**

d *Mrs Ernesta Bortoli is in a medical ward after suffering a stroke. She is going to be transferred to a care home as she can no longer remain in her own home. Deanna Giles, the Ward Nurse, is telephoning The Pines care home to hand over information about Ernesta's ADL score.*

▶10.5 **Listen to the conversation and complete the Katz ADL Index in Exercise 5a using her scores. How much assistance will she need?**

e **In pairs, look at the chart on page 92 and discuss the following questions.**

1 What is assessed using this chart and when is it used?
2 Have you used a chart like this before?
3 Why is it important to note the estimated date of discharge (EDD)?
4 What is a Dosette Box?
5 What can happen if community services are not arranged before patients return home?
6 Why is it important to note the digital door code or the whereabouts of a key?
7 What is a multi-disciplinary team (MDT)?
8 Why is it important to interface with the multi-disciplinary team?
9 Why is it important to discuss discharge plans with the patient or carer?

f *Henry Jacques is an 80-year-old preparing to return home after a total hip replacement. He is a little hard of hearing and uses a hearing aid. His daughter, Stephanie, lives nearby and has a key to his bungalow. She will be available to pick up Mr Jacques when he is ready for discharge. He is very independent but will need some equipment to help him mobilise (a walking frame) and to help with safety in the shower (a shower chair). He will also need a Dosette Box arranged so that he can manage his medications at home. Stephanie leaves him enough prepared meals in the freezer for the week and Henry always goes to Stephanie's for Sunday lunch. Mr Jacques still has a small wound dressing which will be seen to by the District Nurses.*

In pairs, use the chart on page 92 to interview Mr Jacques about his discharge planning needs. Student A, you are the Discharge Planning Nurse; Student B, you are Mr Jacques. Complete all relevant parts of the chart. Remember to speak clearly and check for understanding. Use active listening strategies to show Mr Jacques you are interested in what he has to say. Swap roles and practise again.

Share your knowledge

In small groups, discuss the following questions and then feed back your group's ideas to the class.

- What assessment tools do you use in your country when transferring patients from a hospital to another healthcare facility?
- What are these assessment tools used for?
- Can this process be made more efficient with the use of technology?

Unit 1

2 e

Patient details	
Full name	Margaret Blake
DOB	16 October 1935
Reason for admission	review of a venous ulcer
Past medical history	IDDM (insulin-dependent diabetes mellitus) HT (hypertension) MI four months ago
Past surgical history	femoral-popliteal bypass four months ago
Medication	insulin, half an aspirin and a multivitamin
Allergies	penicillin and codeine
Next of kin	Judy Simpson

5 h

THE ALEXANDRA HOSPITAL

U/N: 619237
Surname: Cummins
Given names: Fred
DOB: 17.02.1955

PATIENT RECORD

DATE & TIME	Add signature, printed name, staff category, date and time to all entries MAKE ALL NOTES CONCISE AND RELEVANT Leave no gaps between entries
20.5.2008 15.30hrs.	Mr Cummins was hypertensive this am BP elevated to 180/100 and P 86 at 10.00hrs. c/o headache. Pt. stated he had no chest pain. Given paracetamol 1g with good effect. Headache relieved. BP checked at 10.30hrs. BP decreased to 150/85, P 77. S Stottle (RN) STOTTLE

6 a/c

THE ALEXANDRA HOSPITAL

U/N: 324710
Surname: Small
Given names: Gladys
DOB: 15.11.1935

OBSERVATION CHART

Date	Time	T	P	R	BP	Comments	Sign name
4/3/08	02.00	36^3	86	18	173/101		J. Plant (RN)
4/3/08	06.00	36^4	75	18	175/95		J. Plant (RN)
4/3/08	10.00	36^4	100	20	210/120		J. Hardcastle (RN)
4/3/08	14.00	36^3	95	18	185/90		J. Hardcastle (RN)
4/3/08	15.00	36^4	76	16	170/85		J. Hardcastle (RN)

Unit 2

6 e

Student A

You are working with a colleague on the evening shift. You have both read Mrs Oondahi's notes. Ask and answer questions about Mrs Oondahi's respiratory status using the prompts.

respiratory rate / at the moment?   how?
how much oxygen?   morphine?

7 e

THE ALEXANDRA HOSPITAL

U/N: 593712
Surname: Castle
Given names: Rebecca
DOB: 15.9.1922   Sex: Female

OBSERVATION CHART

Date	Time	T	P	RR	BP	Pain	Comments	Sign name
4.2.09	06.00	36⁵	72	16	110/70	0/10		M. Potter (RN)
4.2.09	07.00	36⁷	76	18	105/65	0/10		M. Potter (RN)
4.2.09	08.00						OT	
4.2.09	09.00						OT	
4.2.09	10.00						OT	
4.2.09	11.00						OT	
4.2.09	12.00						OT	
4.2.09	13.00						OT	
4.2.09	14.00	36²	78	22	120/75	6/10	RTW on PCA Fentanyl	M. Potter (RN)
4.2.09	15.00	36⁵	76	18	115/65	4/10	PCA Fentanyl	M. Potter (RN)
4.2.09	16.00							

Unit 4

3 g Mr Jim Dunston, a 38-year-old self-employed man has been admitted to the Diabetic Unit for treatment of an ulcer on the underside of his left foot and for a review of his insulin. He is a keen fisherman who often goes rock fishing. During a recent fishing trip, while walking barefoot, he trod on some sharp pieces of rock, injuring his foot. The wound has been very slow to heal and is now infected. He has signs of poor circulation and hypertension. Mr Dunston goes to the local club for a meal most days and tends to have a high intake of alcohol.

Unit 6

8 d

PATIENT'S NAME: _Mrs Elisha Gupta_   U/N: _773546_

MORNING (around 08.00); MIDDAY (between 12.00 & 14.00); EVENING (around 18.00); BEDTIME (around 22.00)

Enter dose against time required. Use only one route for each entry.			REGULAR MEDICATIONS							MONTH _May_				YEAR _2008_
			4.5	5.5	6.5	7.5	8.5	9.5	10.5					
Date ➤	4.5		MEDICINE (Approved Name)			SPECIAL INSTRUCTIONS				PRESCRIBER'S SIGNATURE			Pharmacist S.Newton	
Route ➤	po		_Furosemide_							_F Frankston_			Supply	
Specify time required ▼	Dose 20mg ▼	sign / Dose change ▼								Bleep no: _5690_				
Morning	08.00	40mg												
Midday	12.00	40mg												
Evening														
Bedtime														
NON-ADMINISTRATION CODE:		X Doctor's request		2. Patient not on ward		3. Unable / No access								
		4. Refused		5. Medication not available		6. See notes								

PATIENT'S NAME: _Mr David Albiston_   **U/N:** _133579_

MORNING (around 08.00); MIDDAY (between 12.00 & 14.00); EVENING (around 18.00); BEDTIME (around 22.00)

Enter dose against time required. Use only one route for each entry.			REGULAR MEDICATIONS						MONTH _APRIL_			YEAR _2008_	
			27.4	28.4	29.4	30.4							
Date ➤	27.4		MEDICINE (Approved Name) _Atorvastatin_				SPECIAL INSTRUCTIONS		PRESCRIBER'S SIGNATURE _B.Khan_			Pharmacist S.Newton	
Route ➤	po												
Specify time required ▼	Dose 40mg mane ▼	sign										Supply	
		Dose change ▼							bleep no: 5647				
Morning	08.00	40mg	FM	BN	HN								
Midday													
Evening													
Bedtime													
Enter dose against time required. Use only one route for each entry			REGULAR MEDICATIONS						MONTH _APRIL_			YEAR _2008_	
			29.4										
Date ➤	28.4		MEDICINE (Approved Name) _Multi B Vitamin_				SPECIAL INSTRUCTIONS		PRESCRIBER'S SIGNATURE _S.Tofran_			Pharmacist S.Newton	
Route ➤	po												
Specify time required ▼	Dose 100mg mane ▼	sign										Supply	
		Dose change ▼							Bleep no: 4389				
Morning	08.00	100mg											
Midday													
Evening													
Bedtime													

NON-ADMINISTRATION CODE: X Doctor's request   2. Patient not on ward   3. Unable / No access
                            4. Refused   5. Medication not available 6. See notes

Unit 7

2 d

Mr Zhu
Remove cannula after last
dose of IV ABs
Start on Oral Antibiotics
Monitor temp carefully

4 d

Date of message	
Time of message	
Name of caller	
Nature of call	
Instructions	
Message documented in Patient Record	Yes / Not necessary
Signature of call recipient	

FLUID BALANCE CHART
(Not to be filed in Medical Record)

Name: Miss Judith Stavel
U/N 473652338
Date: 14.11.2009

Bodyweight _____ 72kg _____

24hrs from __01.00__ on __14.11.09__ to __01.00__ on __15.11.09__

INPUT					OUTPUT					
Time	Oral	Amount	IV Fluids	Amount	Vomit	Asp	U/O	Drains	Bowel	
01.00			1L N/S to KVO (42 ml hr) C/F	(900)						
02.00				42						
03.00				42			100			
04.00			1L 5% Dextrose 8/24	125			Wet bed+			
05.00	H₂O	approx 100		125	Lge amt					
06.00			IV ABs +100 ml	225			250			
07.00	tea	20		125						
08.00				125			Wet bed++			
09.00	OJ	150		125					BNO	
10.00	tea	100		125	100 ml					
11.00				125			300			
12.00			1L N/S 8/24	125				60ml	BO mod amt	
13.00				125	60 ml		UTT			
14.00				125						
15.00				125						
16.00				125					BO sml amt	
17.00	H₂O	½ cup		125	Sml amt					
18.00	tea	100	IV ABs + 100 ml	225						
19.00				125						
20.00			1L 5% Dextrose 8/24	125						
21.00	milk	100		125						
22.00	H₂O	50		125						
23.00				125						
24.00				125				55 ml		
TOTAL										

Unit 8

APPENDICECTOMY : WHAT TO EXPECT AFTER YOUR OPERATION

What is appendicitis?
Appendicitis is the inflammation or swelling of the appendix, a small tube on the end of the intestine.

What is an appendicectomy?
An appendicectomy is the name of the operation to remove the appendix.

Will I have a scar?
No, you won't. The operation is performed by passing a laparoscope through your navel and removing the appendix. A laparoscope is a tube-like instrument with a type of camera on the end of it. The surgeon is able to see your appendix through the laparoscope and remove it through the same tube.

Will I have a dressing?
You will have a small dressing over your navel in case there is a small amount of discharge after the operation. If the discharge becomes discoloured and smelly, you will have to take a course of antibiotics to clear the infection.

Will I have a 'drip'?
Yes. When you come back to the ward after your operation you will have an IV infusion, or 'drip', in your arm, just until you are able to drink fluids again.

Will I be able to eat and drink after the operation?
Yes, you will be able to eat a soft diet as soon as the Nursing staff is satisfied that your bowels are working again after the operation.

Will I be in a lot of pain?
Any abdominal surgery can cause some discomfort. You will have patient-controlled analgesia running through the drip in your arm. When you are feeling uncomfortable, you can press a small hand-held control button and you will receive some pain relief through the drip in your arm.

Is there anything else I'll have to do after the operation?
We advise you to continue wearing your anti-embolic stockings until you are up and about again. Keep up the deep breathing exercises too using your tri-ball.

How soon can I get back to my normal activities?
It usually takes a few days to recover from the operation and get back to normal activities. However, make sure you avoid strenuous activity for three to four weeks after the operation.

4 f

Patient questions:

What is appendicitis?

What is an appendicectomy?

Will the operation leave a scar?

Will I have a dressing?

Will I have a drip?

Can I eat and drink after the operation?

Will I be in a lot of pain?

Is there anything else I'll have to do after the operation?

How soon can I get back to my normal activities?

6 a

THE ALEXANDRA HOSPITAL

U/N: 674903

Surname: Mainwaring

Given names: Belinda Anne

DOB: 3.8.1963   Sex: F

Operation or procedure: Rt shoulder arthroscopy and repair of rotator cuff

PATIENT PRE-OPERATIVE CHECKLIST

To be used as an added check so that the patient is fully prepared for his/her visit to the Operating Theatre.

1 To be signed by Nursing staff on completion of patient preparation for Operating Theatre.

2 To be counter-checked by the nurse receiving the patient in the Operating Theatre.

NB: When check is completed, tick the appropriate column.	YES	NO or N/A	O/T
1 Identification bracelet(s) correct and correctly worn x2	✓		
2 Consent form signed			
3 Operation site marked by surgeon			
4 Charts correct, including Drug Chart, Prescription Chart, Notes, Fluid Charts			
5 X-rays included with Charts and Patient Notes			
6 Any known allergies (Red bracelet worn Yes/No)			
7 Caps, crowns, bridges Identify position			
8 Dentures removed (if not removed on ward, please state)			
9 Operation site shaved			
10 Nail varnish removed			
11 Jewellery removed or taped			
12 Identify piercings			
13 Theatre gown worn / anti-embolic stockings / knickers			
14 Pre-med given as per anaesthetic chart			
Urine last voided at _____ am/pm Catheterised at am/pm or N/A			
Fluid last given at _____ am/pm Food last given at _____ am/pm			
Prepared by (Nursing staff – Ward) *VJ Allum (RN)* Date: *30.5.08* Time *11.00*(am)/pm			
Received by (Nursing staff – Theatre) *W McNoughtin (RN)* Date: *30.5.08* Time *11.15*(am)/pm			

Unit 9

1 e

> **Name:** Mr Richard Symons
> **U/N:** 354609
> **Operation:** removal of 2cm² piece of metal from abdomen post industrial accident
> **Post-op complications:** very drowsy, slow to come out of anaesthetic. GCS of 12/15 at 11.00hrs, 13/15 at 11.30hrs
> **Obs. in Recovery:** 11.30hrs Temp 36°, Pulse 70, BP 110/65, SaO₂ 97% on oxygen @ 3L/min
> **IV Therapy:** 1L Normal Saline over 8 hours
> **Nausea and Vomiting:** nil, anti-emetic prn
> **Drains:** one redivac in situ
> **Dressing:** wound closure with clips, NAD intact
> **Pain:** Pethidine 100mg 3 hourly for 3 days, then oral analgesia

6 a

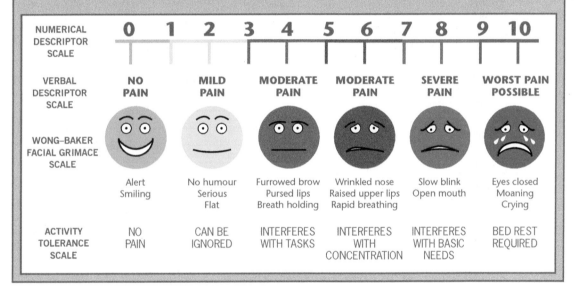

Pain Scales: Universal Pain Assessment Tool

This pain assessment tool is intended to help patient care providers assess pain according to individual patient needs. Explain and use 0–10 scale for patient self-assessment. Use the faces or behavioural observations to interpret expressed pain when patient cannot communicate his/her pain intensity.

NUMERICAL DESCRIPTOR SCALE	0	1	2	3	4	5	6	7	8	9	10
VERBAL DESCRIPTOR SCALE	NO PAIN		MILD PAIN		MODERATE PAIN		MODERATE PAIN		SEVERE PAIN		WORST PAIN POSSIBLE
WONG–BAKER FACIAL GRIMACE SCALE	Alert Smiling		No humour Serious Flat		Furrowed brow Pursed lips Breath holding		Wrinkled nose Raised upper lips Rapid breathing		Slow blink Open mouth		Eyes closed Moaning Crying
ACTIVITY TOLERANCE SCALE	NO PAIN		CAN BE IGNORED		INTERFERES WITH TASKS		INTERFERES WITH CONCENTRATION		INTERFERES WITH BASIC NEEDS		BED REST REQUIRED

Unit 10

2 e Mr Edward Vogel had a left CVA and has moderate right-sided weakness. He lives on his own in a bungalow which will have to be adapted for his current needs: a bathroom adaptation and ramps in place of steps. A home assessment has been arranged for 15 October. His next of kin is an old friend, Eva Sanki. He will need his meals delivered as he cannot manage to cook for himself.

4 d Mr Lachlan suffered a left CVA eight weeks ago, causing a right hemiplegia.
Explain to Mr Lachlan's daughter, Ruth, the effects of a left-sided stroke.

Discharge Plan and checklist – to be commenced on day of admission

Circle multiple choice answer

Patient name: U/N: Address: (addressograph label)	Date of admission: EDD:	Name of carer/relative:	Dosette Box used Yes/No

Home care: community services

Does patient have existing services? Yes/No	Which services? Frequency?	Have they been cancelled? Yes/No or N/A Date:
District Nurse Yes/No	Reason? Frequency?	District Nurse cancelled? Yes/No or N/A Date:
Aids/Adaptions to be put in place for discharge? Yes/No or N/A	Which aids? Include oxygen + nebuliser	Date planned for aids to be in place:

Home circumstances

Accommodation: bungalow / flat / house / care home	Lives alone / carer (relationship and name)	Digital door code: Yes/No Number:	Name of care home: or N/A	House key kept with: or N/A

Multi-disciplinary team referrals

	Date referred	Date seen	Seen by whom	Outcome
Physiotherapist				
Occupational Therapist				
Medical Social Worker				
Clinical Nurse Specialist				
Other				

Prior to discharge

Plans discussed and agreed with Pt./carer Yes/No	Plans discussed and agreed with MDT Yes/No	District Nurse informed Yes/No Date:	Outpatient appointment booked Yes/No or own GP
Equipment/Aids delivered to patient's home Yes/No	Dosette Box required for discharge Yes/No Pharmacy aware Yes/No	Essential food, water, heating in situ in own home Yes/No or N/A	Transport arranged Yes /No

Date _____   Signature of person completing _____

Print name _____   Grade _____

Unit 1

2 d

Patient details	
Full name	Edna May Harris
DOB	13 July 1943
Reason for admission	possible amputation Rt. middle toe
Past medical history	PVD (peripheral vascular disease)
Past surgical history	Rt. femoral angioplasty
Medication	paracetamol x2 four times a day, ferrous sulphate x1 daily
Allergies	N/K (nil known)
Next of kin	Rose Hlavarty

5 h

THE ALEXANDRA HOSPITAL

U/N: 213498
Surname: Lancaster
Given names: Polly
DOB: 14.06.1942

PATIENT RECORD

DATE & TIME	Add signature, printed name, staff category, date and time to all entries MAKE ALL NOTES CONCISE AND RELEVANT Leave no gaps between entries
20.5.2008 05.30hrs.	Mrs Lancaster had a restless night. c/o chest pain at 02.15hrs. Night SHO called. BP 215/105, P 92 at 02.20hrs. ECG ordered and attended by nursing staff. O₂ via mask and GTN sl administered. BP dropped to 180/86 P 82 at 02.40hrs. No c/o further chest pain. L Knight (RN)

Unit 2

6 e

> **Student B**
> You are working with a colleague on the evening shift. You have both read Mrs Oondahi's notes. Ask and answer questions about Mrs Oondahi's respiratory status using the prompts.
>
> comfortable?   trouble / breathing?
> oxygen?   last / pain score?

Unit 4

3 g Ms Sylvia Smythe is a 27-year-old who was diagnosed with Type 1 diabetes after a sudden onset of increased thirst and frequent urination. She had also lost a lot of weight despite having an increased appetite. She has a family history of hypertension and has recently noticed that her blood pressure is quite high. Ms Smythe has been admitted to hospital after experiencing some serious hypoglycaemic attacks. One occurred while she was on the bus going to work. She was very lucky that a young nurse was sitting next to her and recognised the acetone smell of her breath as a symptom of diabetic ketoacidosis. During this hospital admission her insulin use, diet and exercise program will be reviewed.

Unit 7

2 d

Mrs Langley
- Flush cannula with heparin instead of N/S before giving IV ABs
- Give 10° litres instead of 8° litres
- Watch K levels

4 d

Telephone Ward 16C - Mr Henry is booked to have a PICC line inserted tomorrow 10.30 am. He needs a porter to bring him to the IV Infusion Room. Don't forget IV Prescription Chart with him.

Unit 10

4 d Mrs Polansky suffered a right CVA eight weeks ago, causing a left hemiplegia. Explain to Mrs Polansky's daughter, Ewa, the effects of a right-sided stroke.

1.1

Shona: Good morning, Mrs Chad. My name's Shona. I'll be admitting you to the ward today. Would you like to come into the Patient Admission Office so I can get some paperwork done?

Mrs Chad: Good morning, Shona. Yes, thanks, I could do with a sit down.

Shona: Here you are. You take this chair here. You can put your stick on the edge of the chair if you like.

Mrs Chad: Oh. Thank you, dear.

Shona: How are you today?

Mrs Chad: Not too bad, thank you. I haven't been waiting for too long at all.

Shona: That's good. Now, I'm going to be taking down some details before you're admitted to the Cardiac Unit today. I'd like to ask you a few questions, if it's all right with you?

Mrs Chad: Yes, of course. That's fine.

Shona: All right, well now, let me just get the admission form.

1.2

Shona: Right, let's get started. Would you mind if I check out some details first?

Mrs Chad: No, not at all. What would you like to know?

Shona: [smiles] I'd just like to check your name and date of birth and see if your identity bracelet is correct. Can you tell me your full name, please?

Mrs Chad: Yes, it's Doreen Mary Chad and my date of birth is the fifth of June nineteen twenty-three. Quite a while ago, isn't it?

Shona: [smiles and laughs] Not so long ago. Time goes very fast when you're busy, doesn't it? Right now, let's see. Doreen Mary Chad. C-H-A-D. That's correct, isn't it?

Mrs Chad: Yes, that's right. Chad with a 'd'.

Shona: And your date of birth is the fifth of June nineteen twenty-three.

Mrs Chad: Yes.

Shona: All right. Can you tell me why you're here today?

Mrs Chad: Well, um, I've got high blood pressure, and I'm here for some tests. My doctor asked me to come here to see what's going on.

Shona: OK. Now I'd like to ask you about your past medical history. Have you had any serious illnesses in the past?

Mrs Chad: Yes, I had a mild heart attack last year. It was quite frightening.

Shona: [leans towards patient and nods] Yes, I'm sure it was. Now, er, what about past surgical history? Have you ever had any operations?

Mrs Chad: No, I'm very lucky. I never have.

Shona: [smiles] That *is* lucky. Now, are you taking any medications at the moment?

Mrs Chad: Yes, my doctor put me on some blood pressure tablets after my heart attack.

Shona: [nods] Do you know what they're called?

Mrs Chad: I don't know, but I've got them here with me. I was told to bring them.

Shona: Mm. That's good. [smiles] Do you think you can show them to me, please?

Mrs Chad: Yes, I can. I've got them somewhere in my bag. Here they are. I take them in the morning with breakfast.

Shona: Right, that's fine. You're taking metaprolol to lower your blood pressure. I'll just write down the name of the medication on the admission form. Metaprolol. Do you have any allergies to any medications?

Mrs Chad: Not that I know of.

Shona: Um. What about food allergies? Any food which doesn't agree with you?

Mrs Chad: No, no, nothing like that.

Shona: Good. [smiles] Are you allergic to sticking plaster or iodine?

Mrs Chad: No, I've never had any problems before.

Shona: All right. Can you tell me the name of your next of kin?

Mrs Chad: It's my son, Jeremy. Jeremy Chad.

Shona: Thanks. That's all for me. I'll leave you here for a minute while I get the admitting doctor to come and see you. Are you comfortable?

Mrs Chad: Yes, thanks. I'm quite all right here.

1.3

Susanna: Hello, Mr Hockings. I wondered if I could have a chat with you about your blood pressure management before you go home?

Mr Hockings: Hello, Susanna. Yes, sure.

Susanna: Great. I'll just grab a chair. [gets a chair and sits down] Now, you've had a bit of a shock with your blood pressure, haven't you?

Mr Hockings: Yeah, you're right there. I had no idea. I mean I was feeling a bit more tired than usual, and my wife said she noticed that my face was a bit flushed. The thing is that I never thought about blood pressure.

Susanna: Mm, yeah [nods]. That's probably why they call it the 'silent killer'. For most people, the only symptom they have of hypertension is high blood pressure itself.

Mr Hockings: Like you say, it's come as a bit of a shock. So, what do I have to do when I go home? What should I watch for?

Susanna: Well now, remember yesterday we went through the sort of lifestyle changes I'd like you to look at?

Mr Hockings: Yes, I've got all the information about the *Stop Smoking* service, and I've started on the nicotine patches. The dietitian spoke to me yesterday about a healthier diet. My wife even went out and bought a cookbook! We'll both start the exercise programme here at the hospital. Was there anything else?

Susanna: [laughs] I hope the recipe book was for you. I can see you cooking up a storm in the kitchen.

Mr Hockings: I don't know about that. I don't think my wife would agree with you.

Susanna: You did well to remember all the information. It's a lot to take in at once and I'm

really pleased that you're fired up and ready to go. The only other thing that we need to talk about is your blood pressure itself. It would be a good idea to buy a small blood pressure monitor and take your blood pressure regularly. That way you can keep an eye on it yourself. It puts you in charge of your own health. I think that's important, don't you?

Mr Hockings: Yeah, you're right. It's much better that way.

1.4

Emily: Right, now Mrs Cho in bed number five. Mrs Cho was readmitted yesterday because of uncontrolled hypertension. You'll probably remember her from last week. She went home but couldn't manage her ADLs by herself. Her daughter had to come in every morning to give her a shower and help her during the day. She's been quite distressed about it, according to her daughter. She presented to the unit with uncontrolled hypertension, despite a change in medication. She has a past history of MI this year in June. Um, this morning she complained of chest pain. The SHO was called. Her BP at the time – er, that was 10 am – was two ten over one oh five and her pulse was one hundred. She had an ECG done and was given GTN sublingually. We gave her some O$_2$ via the mask and she seemed to settle. She's in for cardiac catheterisation tomorrow to assess the extent of the damage to her heart. I've booked the porter already. Strict fourth hourly obs. BP and pulse and report any chest pain immediately, of course. She's had no chest pain this shift.

1.5

Nick: Mrs Smits complained of chest pain at 10 pm. The SHO was informed. Oxygen was administered via a mask. Her blood pressure was two hundred and twenty over one hundred and her pulse was one hundred and twenty at five past ten. The SHO ordered an ECG, which was done by nursing staff. GTN sublingual was given with good effect. The chest pain was relieved within a couple of minutes.

1.6

Jenny: All right, now I'll just let you know about Mrs Small's BP. As you know, she was admitted just before 2 am yesterday with poorly managed hypertension. She's quite elderly and trying to cope at home, but the previous medication wasn't working well for her at all. Doctor Fielding wants to put her on something else and wants to monitor her BP in hospital over three days. If you look at her Obs. Chart from yesterday, you'll see that she was quite hypertensive on admission. BP was one hundred and seventy three over one hundred and one, pulse eighty-six. At 6 am her BP was about the same, one seventy-five over ninety and pulse seventy-six. During the morning shift at 10 am she shot up to two hundred and ten over one thirty, with a pulse of a hundred and twelve. She had some chest pain, too. Doctor Fielding came up to see her about the chest pain and high BP. He did all the usual things for her ECG, GTN sublingually, and she settled a bit by 2 pm. By two, her BP was one ninety-five over ninety and her pulse was ninety-seven. I took her obs. again at 3 pm, just before handover. She's gone down to one eighty over eighty-five with a pulse of eighty-six. Doctor Fielding's happy with that but just keep an eye on her, will you?

2.1

Eleanor: Good morning, Mrs Drake. How are you?

Mrs Drake: Much better, thank you. My chest feels less tight and I'm breathing much better now.

Eleanor: [smiles] That's great. I'm going to show you how to use a peak flow meter today. Would you mind if I go through it with you now? You'll have to use one regularly to keep an eye on your asthma at home.

Mrs Drake: No, that'll be fine. I'm happy to do anything which will stop me going back into hospital.

Eleanor: Yes, it's much better to manage it at home. Now, I'd like you to use this peak flow meter at the same time every day.

Mrs Drake: Oh, all right. Is that important? I mean, is it important to use it at the same time every day?

Eleanor: Yes, it's so that you can compare the readings. It's better if they're taken at the same time each day.

Mrs Drake: Oh, I see.

Eleanor: Another thing – could you record your readings in this Daily Record Chart, please? I've got one for you here.

Mrs Drake: Right. So I take the peak flow reading at the same time every day and record it in this Daily Record Chart.

Eleanor: [nods] Yes. That's right. You just write the details along the line for that day, like this. Something else which is important is, I'd like you to bring the Daily Record Chart with you every time you come here to the Asthma Clinic.

Mrs Drake: All right, I'll do that. So, just so I know I have it correct: I take the reading every day at the same time, then I write the result on my Daily Record Chart, and I mustn't forget to always bring the chart to the Asthma Clinic. I'll never remember all that!

Eleanor: [smiles] Don't worry, it'll become a habit.

2.2

Eleanor: If you're ready, I'll just show you how to use the peak flow meter. It's easy to use. You just need to follow some simple instructions. I'll go through it with you.

Mrs Drake: All right, thanks.

Eleanor: Right, first of all, just move the red indicator to the bottom of the numbered scale, like this.

Mrs Drake: Yes, I can see where the indicator goes.

Eleanor: Now, stand up. Take a deep breath and try to fill your lungs as much as you can. Like this. Place your lips tightly around the mouthpiece. Could you show me? Yes, that's right. Next, blow as hard and as fast as you can with one breath. Have a go! That's great. Make a note of the final position of the marker. That's your peak flow reading. After that, I want you to blow into the peak flow meter two more times. The last thing to remember is to record the highest of the three readings on your Daily Record Chart.

Mrs Drake: Oh, so I have to do three readings every time?

Eleanor: Yes, that's right. Take three readings but only record the highest on your chart. Do you have any questions?

Mrs Drake: No, I think I've got all that.

2.3

Melanie: Hello, Mr Dwyer. I'd just like to show you how to use this nebuliser. I'll bring a chair up so I can have a chat with you. You haven't used one of these before, have you?

Mr Dwyer: No, this is all new to me. I've been using an inhaler for years now, but this time it just wasn't enough.

Melanie: Well, let's hope you only need the nebuliser for acute attacks. The inhaler should be enough as a regular preventer.

Mr Dwyer: OK. So what do I have to do?

Melanie: Right. Well, I'll go through all the steps with you. It's not too difficult. I'm sure you'll catch on quickly. First of all, fill the chamber of the nebuliser with inhalant medication. The inhalant solution is in these small plastic nebules.

Mr Dwyer: OK, I just put the solution in the chamber here. That's right, isn't it?

Melanie: Yes, that's the right place. Now, attach the tubing to the oxygen outlet on the wall. It's this outlet here, not the other one. That's for something else. That's quite important. Um, are you OK with that?

Mr Dwyer: Right. Yes, I've got that.

Melanie: Next, put on the mask and tighten the elastic straps so that it fits snugly around the head. I'll show you.

Mr Dwyer: Yes, I see. Got it.

Melanie: After that, turn on the oxygen … so the liquid medication turns into a fine mist. I'll just turn it on. You should put it at around six litres.

Mr Dwyer: I see. It's starting to fizz up.

Melanie: Mm. Yes, that's the idea. Finally, inhale the mist until it's finished.

Mr Dwyer: OK. And then I just turn it off?

Melanie: Yep, until the next time. Any questions?

Mr Dwyer: No, I think you've covered everything. Thanks. I think I'll be fine with it.

Melanie: Yes, I'm sure you will. I'll check on you when you're ready for the next dose.

2.4

Tim: Hello, Susie. Can I come and sit here with you for a while? You're looking a bit brighter than yesterday, aren't you? We'll have a chat about your breathing now, and then I'll have a talk to you about what happens to your airways when you have an asthma attack. OK with you?

Susie: Why do I have to do all that? Sounds like school!

Tim: Come on. It's not as bad as that! The thing is, Susie, I want you to be able to understand what's happening to you during an asthma attack, so that you can cope when you have another attack. Does that sound like a good idea?

Susie: Yeah, I suppose so. So what do I have to do?

Tim: Well, I've got this little booklet for you to take home with you. Have a look on the first page, and you'll see a diagram of what we call

your respiratory system. That's the one. Now, I'm going to tell you what happens to the air when it comes into our bodies and travels to our lungs.

Susie: Is that, like, when you're having an asthma attack?

Tim: Good point. No, I'm talking about what happens normally, how the air should move into our lungs.

Susie: Oh, OK.

Tim: Right, let's start. The air is breathed into your nasal cavity – that's your nose – where it's warmed and filtered. It moves past the oral cavity, that's your mouth. Now it goes through your pharynx, or throat, and then comes to the epiglottis. That's the little flap which stops food going into your lungs when you swallow. The tube which carries food to your stomach is right next to it, so that part is like a road which divides into two roads. Can you see that?

Susie: Yeah. Hey, this is interesting!

Tim: Oh, great! I thought you'd find it interesting. Now, the air is moving past your larynx, or voice box, so that you can make sounds. It moves down your trachea, or windpipe, and into the bronchus. That's the part which swells when you have an attack. We'll talk about what happens in an asthma attack later, OK?

Susie: Yeah, OK. What happens to the air now, Tim?

Tim: Oh, I can see you're right into this! Well, see how the bronchus divides into the two lungs? That's it. The lungs are covered by the pleural membrane. That's the special covering that protects your lungs. *Pleural* is just a medical word for lungs. Inside the lungs are the alveoli, which are masses of tiny sacs which help your lungs to exchange carbon dioxide for oxygen. Then you can breathe out the carbon dioxide.

Susie: I get it now. What about these things around the lungs?

Tim: Those are your ribs. In between the ribs we have the intercostal space. *Intercostal* is the medical word for 'in between the ribs'. Well done, Susie. You've got all the labels there.

2.5

Tim: Have a look at the next page for me. Can you see the two diagrams?

Susie: These ones? One says it's a picture of healthy airways and the other is a picture of a person who's having an asthma attack.

Tim: That's right. Let's call this one healthy airways and the other one asthmatic airways. You can see that the healthy airways have a lining of healthy tissue. The tissue layer isn't very thick.

Susie: But the tissue in the asthma airways is thicker, isn't it?

Tim: Yes, the tissue in the asthma airways becomes inflamed.

Susie: What's the layer around the tissue called?

Tim: That's a muscle layer. The muscle layer contracts, or squeezes. In the healthy airways, the air flows through the airways and is conducted into and out of the alveoli, or tiny air sacs. In the alveoli, carbon dioxide is exchanged with oxygen. This is called respiration, or breathing.

Susie: What happens to the other airway – I mean, to the asthmatic airway?

Tim: You remember that the tissue in the asthma airways becomes swollen during an asthma attack?

Susie: Yeah.

Tim: Well, the muscle squeezes the swollen tissue and the lining of the airways swells as well. This means the airway is narrowed. Can you see that there is less room for air to go through?

Susie: Yeah, I can see that.

Tim: That's why your chest muscles tighten and it becomes difficult to breathe. You start wheezing when you breathe in. It also takes much longer for you to breathe out again.

Susie: I hate that!

Tim: It's frightening when it happens, isn't it? Now that you know what happens during an asthma attack, it'll make it easier for you to understand why you need your medication.

Susie: Yeah, thanks, Tim. I'll look at the book until mum comes back.

 2.6

1

Now to Mr Frank. Mr Frank is really at a terminal stage now. His pain was not relieved by morphine 5mg via continuous infusion. The morphine was increased to 10mg, and this seems to be holding the pain now. Mr Frank's respiratory rate is depressed since the increase in the morphine rate via the subcutaneous pump, but this is to be expected. Just keep him comfortable tonight, please. His family will stay with him all night in the single room.

2

This is Judy Brown in bed 17. I'll just get her charts so I can show you what's been happening today. OK. Here they are. She came back to the ward at 11 with a PCA with morphine running post-op. I'll check the settings with you in a moment, but I just wanted to be sure you know to monitor Judy's respirations second hourly as per the Clinical Pathway. OK, so let's go through these settings.

3

Hello, it's Barbara from Ward 15 here. Are you the physio on call this weekend? Oh, good. Look, I thought I'd let you know before you came up to the ward. Mr Walker was very breathless this morning, but it was helped by oxygen at four litres per minute via the nasal cannulae. He may not feel able to have any physio today. Do you still want to come up and see him? Mm, OK, that's a good idea. I'll tell him you'll be up tomorrow morning instead. Thanks. Bye.

4

I'll just explain to you what's happening with your husband's breathing. Mr Sims has a fast respiratory rate at the moment, which is caused by the lung infection he's had for the past few weeks. He has very laboured inspiration and expiration, which is why I've given him some oxygen.

2.7

Mandy: Hi, Rosa. Do you mind if I go through Mrs Castle's chart with you before I go on a break? There are a few things to do while I'm gone, if you don't mind.

Rosa: That's OK, I don't mind. Mrs Castle's on hourly resps, isn't she?

Mandy: Yeah, that's right. She's had a history of respiratory problems, and she became quite breathless after her operation yesterday. In any case, we're still doing hourly resps while she's on PCA fentanyl for pain.

Rosa: Uh-huh OK, right. How's her respiratory rate now?

Mandy: Um, you can see her pre-op resps at 6 am were eighteen. That's about normal for her. I checked her resps at 7 am before she went to Theatres and they were still eighteen.

Rosa: Mm. When did she come back from the operation?

Mandy: She came back a couple of hours ago, at, um, 2 pm. She was in a lot of pain. She scored seven out of ten on the pain score, and she was quite breathless. Her resps went up to twenty-six. I started her on some oxygen at five litres per minute for an hour between 2 and 3 pm because of her breathlessness.

Rosa: Mm, OK. Yes, I see. It looks like she's settled down a bit since then. The fentanyl will have kicked in. I can see her pain score at 3 pm was four out of ten. That's better.

Mandy: Yeah, I just did her obs. a few minutes ago at 3 pm and her resps were down to twenty so that's better too. I've put the oxygen back to three litres per minute.

Rosa: OK. I'll keep an eye on her while you're on your tea break.

Mandy: Thanks. I'll be back in half an hour. I'll do her 4 pm obs. then.

Rosa: OK.

3.1

Sophie: Hi.

Ali: Hi, Sophie. Thanks for coming up to the ward. It's about Mr Jones in bed five. Would you mind giving me some advice on his wound care management?

Sophie: Yeah, sure. Can you fill me in on his past history first?

Ali: Um, right. Mr Jones is a 68-year-old smoker with a long history of PVD. He developed a venous ulcer on his right ankle after he tripped on some stairs at the back of his house. That was, er, about six months ago. His local doctor had a look at it and asked the District Nurses to come and dress the wound at home. Um, they've been dressing the wound three times a week. At that stage it was hoped that he could avoid coming into hospital. He lives with his wife who needs quite a lot of help as she has chronic asthma. It puts quite a lot of strain on her if he has to be hospitalised.

Sophie: Right, that's difficult, isn't it? Obviously the ulcer didn't improve at home, so what happened next?

Ali: Um. Two weeks ago he was admitted to this ward to have an assessment of his circulation and to monitor his wound management. He had a Doppler test done, er, last week which indicated poor blood circulation in his lower legs. Um, he's also been spiking temperatures and the surrounding skin of the wound has become quite reddened. We sent a wound swab off, and we just got the results yesterday. Of course, he's growing a few bugs so he's started on some IV antibiotics.

We're unsure of the best wound management for him. What would you recommend that we change to?

Sophie: Hm, let me have a look at the wound and we'll see what the best option is.

3.2

Sophie: Hello, Mr Jones. My name's Sophie. I'm the wound management Clinical Nurse Specialist here.

Mr Jones: Oh. Hello, Sophie.

Sophie: I believe you've been having a rough time with your leg wound? Would you mind if I have a quick look at it?

Mr Jones: No, no, no, I don't mind.

Sophie: Now, while I take this dressing off, tell me how you've been managing at home.

Mr Jones: Oh, well, you know, it's a bit hard on the wife. She doesn't cope with things very well. I've been doing most of the things around the house for the past few years, but I can't do much now. I've had a difficult time with this wound. I've tried my best, but I just can't do it on my own. What do you think I should do with this ulcer?

Sophie: Well, I think the first thing to do is to reassess the wound. Sometimes you have to come into hospital to get back on track with treatment. OK, Ali, I think that we need to use a different type of dressing method on the wound.

Ali: Right. What do you suggest we use?

Sophie: Er, I'd like to use a VAC dressing on this wound.

Mr Jones: Oh. Sounds nasty.

Sophie: Mr Jones, it's called a VAC, which means Vacuum Assisted Closure, but it's only a gentle suction on the wound.

Mr Jones: I see. Do you think it's a good idea to try that instead of the dressing that they're using now?

Sophie: Yes. I think it'll help the wound heal faster.

Mr Jones: All right. Sounds like a good idea.

Sophie: Would you mind if I covered your wound with a dressing towel for now, while I set up the new dressing?

Mr Jones: No, no, I don't mind. You take your time.

3.3

John Simpkins: Good morning, everyone. Morning. Thanks for coming to the session on wound bed preparation this morning. I think you've all got the handouts, yes? Good, OK. First of all, I'd like to talk about the aim of wound bed preparation and then the barriers to wound healing. Now, I'm sure all of you have had experience with care of different types of wounds. As you probably know, wound bed preparation is an important part of the way wounds are managed these days. The preparation of the wound bed – in other words, the base of the wound – is vital if healing is to take place. I know you'll agree with me that wounds which are resistant to treatment are very frustrating, not least to the patient. The aim of wound bed preparation is to prepare a stable wound environment which results in wound healing. This is achieved by restoring a well-vascularised wound bed, or wound base, so that good blood circulation is achieved and the tissues are supplied with oxygen and other nutrients. It's also important to decrease the high bacterial load by controlling inflammation or infection. In addition, it's necessary to create moisture balance in the wound environment, so that the wound is neither too dry nor too moist. Studies show that wounds will not heal if there are certain barriers to healing present. Er, the first barrier to healing is the presence of necrotic tissue – in other words, dead tissue. The necrotic tissue stops healthy tissue from growing, so it's important to remove any dead tissue from the wound. After necrosis, the second barrier to good healing is, um, high bacterial load, or a high level of infection which is carried by the tissues. It's therefore important that any infections are treated before effective wound care can start. Finally, imbalance of moisture levels in the wound bed also stops the healing process. Wounds with excessive exudate – that is, wounds which are too moist and also wounds which have excessive dryness or desiccation – will not heal properly.

3.4

John Simpkins: Right, I'd like to talk about TIME now. TIME is an acronym for a framework which helps to identify barriers to healing in the wound bed and identifies expected outcomes of treatment. The acronym TIME stands for tissue, infection, moisture balance and edges of the wound. Looking at the tissue factor first, the tissue is not viable if there are still areas of necrosis in the wound. This means that the tissues of the wound bed do not have sufficient blood supply to survive. Debridement of necrotic tissue is necessary to prepare the wound for healing. This is often a surgical procedure, especially if large amounts of necrotic tissue have to be removed. The expected outcome is a wound bed which is well-vascularised and has a good blood supply. The second factor to consider is whether inflammation or infection is present. The aim is to remove the infection and reduce the bacterial load. This is done by using antimicrobial dressings as well as antibiotic medication. Reduced inflammation around the wound is the expected outcome. Next, the moisture imbalance of the wound is treated. Excessive exudate, or discharge of fluid from the wound, causes maceration, or softening, of the wound edges. On the other hand, desiccation, or excessive dryness, also slows healing. In order to restore the moisture balance, it's necessary to use hydrating dressings which add moisture to dry wounds. Negative pressure dressings, for example VAC dressings, remove excess fluid in macerated wounds. The expected outcome is that the wound will have an optimal moisture balance. Finally, if the edge of the wound does not heal or advance, the wound becomes a chronic wound. It then becomes necessary to reassess the wound. During reassessment, different wound management needs to be considered. An example of this is a skin graft, which is used to replace damaged skin. The desired result is that the edge of the wound will advance and heal.

3.5

Krisztina: Hello, Gary, isn't it? I'm Krisztina and this is Judy.
Judy: Hi.
Krisztina: How are you doing?
Gary: Not too bad now. I've had something for the pain, so it's bearable now.
Krisztina: That's good. You've had a tetanus shot, too, I see. We'll clean up the wound for you now. I'll leave you with Judy and she'll do the dressing for you.
Gary: OK, thanks. It looks pretty awful, doesn't it?
Judy: Mm, it was a nasty bite, especially with those puncture wounds. Krisztina, what do you suggest I clean the wound with?
Krisztina: It's best to flush it with lots of Normal Saline before you do the dressing. We do that first, Gary, because it reduces the risk of infection. Even though only fifteen to twenty per cent of dog bites get infected, puncture wounds like yours have a greater chance of infection. You'll be prescribed some antibiotics to take at home, too.
Gary: Um. Speaking of going home, can you give me some advice on looking after this at home?
Krisztina: Sure. The wound will be left open, um, it won't be sutured, Gary, because it heals better if it's left open not stitched closed. I'd like you to keep the dressing clean and dry and come to Outpatients to have the dressing changed daily. I'll get you an appointment card while Judy's doing the dressing for you.
Gary: Mm, all right. What should I do about the antibiotics?
Krisztina: You'll be prescribed some antibiotics by the doctor a bit later. You'll get a script which you can take to the hospital pharmacy to be filled. Make sure you take the whole course of the antibiotics. That's very important. Is there anything else you were concerned about?
Gary: Oh, just one thing. Um, should I get a medical certificate? It looks like I might be off work for a couple of days.
Krisztina: Yes, that'd be a good idea. I'll ask the doctor on duty to write one for you.

3.6

Jennifer: OK, moving on to Gary, um, Gary Stephens in bed 17. Does everyone know Gary? He was attacked in the street by a dog two weeks ago. Initially he went to A&E and was treated there. He had some deep puncture wounds in his left calf and was in a lot of pain.
Brian: The dog bit him twice, didn't it?
Jennifer: Yeah, and it bit him quite deeply. As I said, he went to A&E, um, the wound wasn't sutured but kept open as per the protocol for dog bites with puncture wounds. Gary was given a tetanus shot and sent home with instructions to come to the dressing clinic every day to have the dressing changed. Unfortunately, he tried to do it himself and now he has an infection in the wound and has been admitted to hospital for treatment. Actually, it's quite a bad infection. The wound smells quite a bit.
Brian: So what are we doing with the wound now?

Jennifer: Right. Um, he had a wound review yesterday, as the wound had to be reassessed. The edges weren't healing because of the infection. The wound is quite sloughy, too, but it isn't necrotic. The surrounding skin is a little inflamed so he was started on IV antibiotics yesterday. It was decided to debride the wound in line with wound bed preparation guidelines. You all went to the CPD session on that last week, didn't you?
Felicity: Yeah, everyone went and I've put the guidelines up in the Treatment Room.
Jennifer: Oh, that's good. He went, uh, this morning for a surgical debridement of the wound and came back around 2 pm. He's feeling OK after the debridement; it's not too sore. Ah, there's a small amount of purulent ooze. There's just a little pus in the centre of the wound. The wound has an antimicrobial dressing over it, which is to remain intact until tomorrow. After that, it'll need a daily dressing, please.
Brian: OK, that's good. And he'll have an assessment by the Vascular Team on Monday, right?
Jennifer: Yes, that's right.

4.1

Susan: Good morning, Mrs Kim. My name's Susan. I'll be working out your diabetes management plan with you today.
Mrs Kim: Hello, Susan. Pleased to meet you.
Susan: Come on through to the clinic. This is your first visit here, isn't it?
Mrs Kim: Yes, it's my first time at this clinic. I was in hospital last week and they referred me here after I was discharged. I'd had a few problems controlling my diabetes at home.
Susan: Oh dear, that's a shame, but I'm sure we'll be able to sort something out today. The main purpose of your visit here today is to develop a Personal Care Plan for you. I'd like to fill you in about the way we work here, as you may not be familiar with the Primary Care Team.
Mrs Kim: Oh, no. I've never heard of that. How is it different from what I did before?
Susan: The main difference is that we are building what we call a Practice Team between us here at the Diabetic Clinic, your local doctor and, most importantly, you.
Mrs Kim: Oh, yes, that is a bit different. My local doctor was the only person who looked after me before I started at the Diabetic Clinic.
Susan: Mm. My job is to ensure that there is a good communication network set up so that we can keep track of any changes in your diabetes before they become a problem.
Mrs Kim: That would be good. If only I'd known about this before, maybe I could've avoided the last hospital admission. I was doing so well and then I just seemed to go downhill fast.
Susan: Mm. Yes, that would be frustrating. What happened?
Mrs Kim: Well, I got very run down, and I didn't watch my diet.
Susan: Well, these things can happen.
Mrs Kim: Yes, well, I ended up in hospital because I couldn't control my blood sugar level at home.

Susan: Mm, I see. Well, let's have a look at your routine at home. Can I ask you a few questions?

Mrs Kim: Sure.

4.2

Marta: Hello, Mr Williams. Good to see you again.

Mr Williams: Hello, Marta.

Marta: I'd like to talk to you today about lifestyle and nutrition. You'll have to make some major lifestyle changes if you're going to avoid nasty complications of diabetes.

Mr Williams: All right. I know I haven't been looking after my health lately. I've put on a bit of weight.

Marta: Mm, how many meals a day do you eat?

Mr Williams: It depends. Sometimes I skip meals. I just can't be bothered.

Marta: Yeah, I know it must be difficult for you, but it's important that you eat small, regular meals. You need to reduce your intake of saturated fats. Try to make sure you include carbohydrates in each meal.

Mr Williams: Oh, I know. My daughter is always on about that, too. I bet I know what the next question is.

Marta: OK, it's about weight control. You really should keep a close eye on your weight. How often do you exercise?

Mr Williams: Not enough these days. I used to walk along the beach with my wife.

Marta: Mm, you told me last time that you'd stopped. Could you try to include some physical activity in your daily routine? It would be a good idea to get back to walking along the beach again.

Mr Williams: Yes, I suppose so. All right, I'll make an effort to do that. Any other changes?

Marta: Yes, I've just got a couple more. What's your alcohol intake like? How many drinks do you have per week?

Mr Williams: I used to have a couple of beers in the evening, but I have been having a few more these days.

Marta: Well, look, alcohol in moderation isn't normally a problem. It can be a problem for diabetics, though. You must keep a close eye on your alcohol intake because it can affect your insulin dose.

Mr Williams: Oh, all right. I'll keep an eye on it, as you say. Otherwise it creeps up on you, doesn't it?

Marta: Yes, it does. Last question, it's an important one. How many cigarettes are you smoking at the moment?

Mr Williams: A couple of packs a week. I know, I know. I'm trying to give up.

Marta: Good for you. It is hard but it is important to stop smoking if you want to avoid circulation problems.

Mr Williams: I certainly don't want anything like that.

Marta: It's quite hard to quit on your own. You might like to speak to your doctor about some nicotine patches.

Mr Williams: Thanks, I'll keep that in mind.

4.3

Nadia: Now the normal pancreas produces a hormone called insulin in the beta cells. Insulin regulates blood sugar levels by moving glucose from the blood into muscle, fat and liver cells. The glucose can then be used as fuel for the body.

Beth: Mm. Right. Now what happens when a person has diabetes?

Nadia: Well, the diabetic pancreas either produces no insulin at all in the beta cells, or too little insulin to normalise blood sugar levels. Type 1 diabetes is usually found in children, so you may know it as juvenile diabetes. It occurs when no insulin is produced. People with Type 1 diabetes have to have daily injections of insulin.

Beth: I see. Now what about Type 2 diabetes?

Nadia: It's much more common than Type 1. Actually, it makes up around ninety per cent of all cases. The pancreas produces too little insulin to keep blood sugar levels normal. You may have heard it called mature-onset diabetes or non-insulin-dependent diabetes.

Beth: Oh yes, I think I have.

Nadia: Right, well, actually people of any age can develop Type 2 diabetes and although it's called non-insulin-dependent diabetes, the treatment can include insulin. Of course, diet modification and oral hypoglycaemic medication is tried first, but sometimes it's necessary to have insulin injections. You probably know that it isn't possible to get insulin in an oral form.

Beth: Yes, I know that, but I've been reading about new technology. What was it? Oh yes, insulin inhalers and insulin pumps.

Nadia: Mm, yes, they are looking very promising. The inhalers look like asthma inhalers, and the pumps are quite convenient because you don't have to use a needle every time you need your insulin.

4.4

Nadia: There are basically three options for giving yourself your daily dose of insulin.

Beth: Oh, great. I didn't realise there were any options.

Nadia: Yes, there are. There's been quite a lot of research into giving diabetics the easiest, most convenient way of taking their daily insulin. OK, let's look at the first option. This one is worn on the body all the time, that's night and day. It's an insulin pump.

Beth: How do they work?

Nadia: They deliver a steady flow of insulin throughout the day. They can push through both rapid and short-acting insulin – it doesn't matter which – through a catheter which is placed under the skin.

Beth: I see. So you wouldn't be giving yourself a needle every time.

Nadia: No, you wouldn't. That's one advantage of the technology. The other upside is that it can give you an extra, or bolus, dose to cover those times when you eat more carbohydrate, for example during a meal or a snack. The real advantage of this is that patients have fewer large swings in blood glucose levels. The main disadvantage is the cost. It's the most expensive option.

Beth: Mm. OK. What other options are there?

Nadia: The second option is insulin with an insulin syringe. Insulin is drawn up from a vial into a disposable syringe. This means that the dose required can be drawn up, and varying doses can be drawn up if needed.

Beth: Would that be, say, if you'd eaten a little extra treat that day?

Nadia: Could be. Also, one or two types of insulin can be mixed in the syringe as long as you follow the rule: cloudy insulin before clear insulin.

Beth: Right. The markings on the side of the syringe look quite small, don't they?

Nadia: Mm, the markings are difficult to see, which makes drawing up accurate doses more difficult. It's the cheapest option but the least convenient.

Beth: Right.

Nadia: That leads us to option three. It's called an insulin pen. This one has an insulin cartridge which fits into the device and can be changed when it's finished. There are also pre-filled devices which are disposable and easier for diabetics who have arthritis or are visually impaired.

Beth: They would be much easier to use, wouldn't they?

Nadia: Yes, they're much easier to use and more convenient than syringes. They can even fit into your pocket and look like the real thing! You do still need a needle with this one. The needle is inserted on the end of the device and changed with each injection.

Beth: I see, and I suppose you still have to store the insulin in the same way? It has to be stored in the fridge, doesn't it?

Nadia: Any unopened insulin can be stored in the fridge, just don't let it freeze. Once the insulin is opened it can last up to thirty days if it's kept at a temperature of less than thirty degrees.

Beth: That's easy to remember. Thirty degrees for thirty days. Thanks, Nadia.

4.5

Peter: Christie, I'd like to tell you about Alice Wilson. Alice came to the ward yesterday. She's been having a few hypos at home, so she's in for some investigations.

Christie: She's in bed twelve, isn't she?

Peter: That's right. 85-year-old with a history of Type 2 diabetes controlled with diet and medication. She's on insulin bd while she's in here for stabilisation. Er, she's poorly compliant with her diet, though.

Christie: Ah. That's right, I remember her. She can't give up her cakes and pastries.

Peter: Yeah, it's always been a problem for her. I think we'll have to give her some more diabetes education this admission.

Christie: Mm. So what's happening with her BSLs?

Peter: Right, well, she's on qds plus 2 am BSLs. We've been quite strict about the times we take her blood sugar levels.

Christie: Right, I can see that. Um, 7.30 am before breakfast, 11.30 am before lunch, um, 4.30 pm before dinner. Dinner comes at 5 pm on this ward, doesn't it?

Peter: Mm, that's right. We take the last one at 9.30 pm before bed time and, of course, the 2 am reading.

Christie: Oh. OK. Yes, I see. What should her blood sugar reading be?

Peter: Her BSLs should be between four and eight millimols before meals and less than ten millimols around one and a half hours after meals.

Christie: I see. What about in the evening at bed time? What should it be then?

Peter: It should be around eight millimols around bed time.

Christie: What are Mrs Wilson's readings?

Peter: I'll go through her readings from yesterday first. You can see here at 2 am yesterday her BSL was four point eight. Before breakfast it was five point two.

Christie: Mm, 2 am four point eight and 7.30 am five point two. She had a urinalysis done at 7.30 am, too?

Peter: That's right. It was negative for glucose and ketones. Unfortunately, when her breakfast came she just picked at it and hardly ate anything. Then she raced around trying to get to the shower before anyone else. You can imagine what happened! She had a hypo at 9 am and it went down to one point eight.

Christie: Yeah, I see. Lemonade given and it went up to four point one.

Peter: Mm. That's right. I gave her some lemonade and a sweet biscuit and checked her BSL again at, um, 11.30 am her BSL was fine, five point seven. At 4.30 pm it was seven point one. We were quite pleased about that but in the evening, at 9.30, it was up to fifteen.

Christie: Oh no! What happened?

Peter: It turns out that a well-meaning friend brought her a box of her favourite chocolates. The friend didn't even realise that Alice was a diabetic.

Christie: That's incredible! I suppose it is difficult when you love chocolate.

Peter: I know it's hard for her but something will have to be done about it or she won't be able to manage at home. I rang the Diabetes Educator and she said she'll see her tomorrow. I've also asked the dietitian to see her so we can try to sort out what she does like eating. That may encourage her to eat regular meals.

Christie: Are we testing her urine for ketones at the moment?

Peter: Yeah, while she's having the hypos we're doing a daily urinalysis for ketones.

Christie: And?

Peter: Her urine's been negative for ketones yesterday and today.

Christie: All right. How was she today?

Peter: Much better, as you can see. At 2 am her BSL was still quite high, at eight point zero.

Christie: Well, that was to be expected, wasn't it?

Peter: Yeah. It was six point five at 7.30 and five point two at 11.30. We made sure that she ate her breakfast today and didn't rush to the shower.

Christie: I see she's back on track now. A BSL of five point nine at 4.30 pm and four point eight at 9.30 tonight.

Peter: Yeah, that's right. Her 2 am BSL should be fine, I'd say. She hasn't had any hypos today at all.

Christie: Thanks. I'll keep an eye on her tonight, though.

▇▇ **5.1**

Frances: I'll just pull the curtains around so we can have a private chat. Now, how are you today, Mrs Faisal?

Mrs Faisal: Not too bad, only I've got a lot of problems, er, when I go to the toilet.

Frances: Mm. Do you mean it hurts to pass urine?

Mrs Faisal: Yes. That's right.

Frances: Yes, the morning nurse mentioned something about it during handover. Tell me what happens when you pass urine.

Mrs Faisal: It, um, burns when I go to the toilet, and I have to go all the time.

Frances: Right. So what you're saying is that it hurts when you're actually passing the urine, and you feel like you have to pass urine frequently? Is that right?

Mrs Faisal: Yes. It hurts when the urine comes out, and it's worse because I feel I have to go to the toilet so often.

Frances: I know what you mean. It sounds like you might have a urinary tract infection.

Mrs Faisal: Oh. What did you call it? A urinary ... what was it?

Frances: Its full name is urinary tract infection. We usually call it UTI for short. Have you ever heard of a UTI before?

Mrs Faisal: Yes, I've heard of it, I think.

Frances: I'll phone your doctor about it in a minute. He'll want you to do a urine specimen to send to the Pathology Laboratory for a Culture and Sensitivity Test. That's a test to see if there is any infection in your urinary tract. Dr Sinclair will probably start you on some antibiotics if the results from the lab show you've got an infection.

Mrs Faisal: OK. So you want me to do a urine specimen, do you?

Frances: Yes, that's right. I need to get an MSU, or midstream urine specimen. Some people call it a clean-catch specimen, because you have to collect a urine sample from the middle part of your urine stream. It's better than collecting a sample from the beginning of the urine stream, because there's less contamination.

Mrs Faisal: Less contamination?

Frances: Yes, the sample is less likely to have bacteria from the outside of your urethra. I'll go and get everything you need to do the MSU, and I'll be back in a minute to explain how to do it.

Mrs Faisal: OK, thanks.

▇▇ **5.2**

Frances: All right, here we are. I've brought everything you need to do the MSU. I've got a sterile specimen container for the urine specimen and some disposable wipes.

Mrs Faisal: OK. So what do I do?

Frances: Firstly, wash your hands thoroughly. Then you need to clean the area around the urethra from front to back with these disposable wipes. Right, so step one is?

Mrs Faisal: Ah, the first thing is to wash my hands and then clean the area around my urethra with these disposable wipes.

Frances: Mm, that's it. You need to make sure the area is clean so the urine specimen doesn't get contaminated with any bacteria from the outside.

Mrs Faisal: Right. Then what do I have to do?

Frances: Then, take the lid off the specimen container like this. Don't touch the inside of the container when you take the lid off, or the urine specimen will be contaminated by any bacteria on your hands. Do it like this so that you keep your fingers away from the edge. Don't touch any part in here – I mean, inside the specimen container. Do you see what I mean?

Mrs Faisal: Yes, I see. That's quite important, isn't it?

Frances: Yes, it is. That's to avoid contamination from bacteria on your hands. Can you show me how you'll hold the specimen jar?

Mrs Faisal: Sure. I'll take it like this, and take the lid off without touching the inside.

Frances: That's great. It's so important to do the test correctly, otherwise we'll get a false reading. Now, pass some urine into the toilet and then pass a small amount of urine into the sterile container. Try to catch the middle part of the urine stream. That's why it's called a midstream urine specimen. Do you understand what I mean?

Mrs Faisal: Yes, I think so. Let me repeat what I have to do so I'm sure I've got it right. I pass some urine into the toilet and then some more urine into the container.

Frances: Yes, that's exactly what I want you to do. We want to get the middle part of the stream of urine. Just one more thing – tighten the lid before you give me the specimen container, please.

Mrs Faisal: Oh right, I can see why that's important.

Frances: Mm. I'll send the urine off to the lab straight away, and we'll get the results tomorrow afternoon. Is that explanation clear or would you like to ask any questions?

Mrs Faisal: No, thanks. I understand. I'll go and do that for you now.

Frances: Just before you do the MSU, could you repeat back the steps for me so I can be sure you followed my explanation?

Mrs Faisal: Yes, of course. First I ...

▇▇ **5.3**

Frances: Hello, is that Dr Sinclair?

Dr Sinclair: Yes, it is

Frances: Oh hello, it's Frances from 8 West here. I'm calling about one of your patients, Mrs Faisal.

Dr Sinclair: Er, Mrs Faisal? Can you remind me?

Frances: Yeah, she was admitted two days ago, er ...

Dr Sinclair: Yeah, I remember. Isn't she in for the removal of an ovarian cyst?

Frances: Yeah, that's the patient. I think she may have a UTI. She's complaining of frequency, urgency and pain when she passes urine.

Dr Sinclair: Right. Is she febrile?

Frances: Yeah, her temp's up a bit. She's around thirty-seven point eight. She doesn't feel brilliant either – general malaise.

Dr Sinclair: OK. She's got frequency, urgency, pain and she's febrile. Can you take an MSU and I'll come over and write up some antibiotics.

Frances: The MSU's already done, but I'll leave the Pathology Form at the desk to be signed. Then we can send it to Pathology. I've encouraged her to increase her fluid intake, too.

Dr Sinclair: Great, thanks. I'm just on 8 East at the moment. I'll probably be up there in fifteen minutes.

Frances: Thanks. See you.

▬ 5.4

Mr Zelnic: What happens if the kidneys stop working properly?

Everson: If the kidneys stop working properly, renal, or kidney, disease could be the result. Um, kidney disease is also called renal disease. The nephrons in the kidneys don't function properly and your kidney becomes damaged.

Mr Zelnic: You mean the filtration tubes?

Everson: Ah, yes. The nephrons filter out the waste products in the blood. If the nephrons don't filter properly, the waste products aren't removed. Eventually, toxic levels of waste products build up in the blood.

Mr Zelnic: What about the urine?

Everson: At first, the output of urine drops.

Mr Zelnic: You mean what I've had? I pass very little urine at the moment.

Everson: Yes. It's called oliguria – when there's a low output of urine. Oliguria can be a symptom of the early stage of renal failure. If the kidney disease is untreated, the nephrons stop working altogether and no urine is passed at all. That's called anuria, which means no urine.

Mr Zelnic: Wouldn't that be serious?

Everson: Yes, it is. Um, if your kidneys stop working completely, your body can't get rid of extra water and waste products. Because your kidneys aren't filtering out waste products or excess water, your hands or feet may swell; this build-up of fluid is called oedema. Ah, you may also feel lethargic because your blood hasn't been cleaned and can't function properly. This stage is known as end stage renal failure. Unfortunately, there's no treatment at this stage of kidney disease. People with end stage renal failure have to go on dialysis or perhaps even have a renal transplant.

Mr Zelnic: So how does the doctor know what's going on with my kidneys?

Everson: You may not have any symptoms during the early stages of kidney disease, but there's a blood test which you'll have to check how well the nephrons are filtering. We also do a simple urine test to check for proteinuria, or protein in the urine. It's called a …

▬ 5.5

Everson: It's called a urinalysis and gives some idea of the health of your kidneys. I'd just like you to do it now, if that's all right.

Mr Zelnic: Sure. What do I have to do?

Everson: Um, I've brought you a urinal – a bottle – for the next time you need to pass urine. Here it is. Ah, I just need an ordinary sample of urine.

Mr Zelnic: Oh. OK. In the bottle? You don't want it in a special container?

Everson: No, no, the urinal is fine. I use a disposable dipstick to test the urine. It only takes a few minutes to get a reading. It doesn't have to be sterile and I don't have to send the specimen away. I can do the test here on the ward.

Mr Zelnic: So it's not like that other test I did when I had to be careful not to touch the inside of the container.

Everson: That's right. That was an MSU which I sent to the lab to be tested for the presence of infection. You had to be careful not to contaminate the urine specimen for that one. This is different.

Mr Zelnic: Right. I know I'll have to do a lot of tests. What did you say you are testing for this time?

Everson: Oh, I'm checking for proteinuria; ah, that just means protein in the urine.

Mr Zelnic: I didn't know protein could be in my urine.

Everson: Um, protein shows up in the urine during kidney disease.

Mr Zelnic: Ah, I see.

Everson: We also check for haematuria, or blood in the urine, as it can also indicate that there may be a problem in your kidneys. And we check the pH of your urine, to see if it's alkaline or acidic.

Mr Zelnic: That's too technical for me. I'll give you the urine sample right away if you like.

Everson: Thanks, Mr Zelnic. Um, just ring when you want me to collect it.

▬ 5.6

1 I'd like you to do it now, if that's all right.
2 I need an ordinary sample of urine.
3 It takes a few minutes to get a reading.
4 I'm checking for proteinuria; that means protein in the urine.
5 Ring when you want me to collect it.

▬ 5.7

1 I'd just like you to do it now, if that's all right.
2 I just need an ordinary sample of urine.
3 It only takes a few minutes to get a reading.
4 I'm checking for proteinuria; that just means protein in the urine.
5 Just ring when you want me to collect it.

▬ 5.8

Jo: Did you buzz, Mrs Kastel?

Mrs Kastel: Yes. Nurse, I'm really uncomfortable here, um, I haven't been able to use this bedpan at all.

Jo: OK. You mean that you haven't been able to pass any urine?

Mrs Kastel: No, I haven't been able to go for ages.

Jo: All right. Let me have a look. I'll just close the curtains. Do you mind if I feel your bladder?

Mrs Kastel: No, that's all right.

Jo: How does it feel here?

Mrs Kastel: Ow. Oh, it's quite uncomfortable.

Jo: Mm, your bladder is quite distended. OK. Now, you've still got some urinary retention after your operation, haven't you?

Mrs Kastel: You mean that I can't go to the toilet?

Jo: Yes, that's right. I might have to put in a catheter to drain the urine.

Mrs Kastel: Is that the tube which goes into your bladder? I've seen a few around. You have to carry a bag around with you.

Jo: Yes, that's it. The bag collects the urine. We call them indwelling catheters, or IDCs for short. I've got one here to show you. An indwelling catheter just means a tube which is left in situ – I mean, left in place. The tube is inserted through the urethra and goes into your bladder. I inflate the little balloon on the end, this one here, with water, and it sits at the neck of your bladder. We have to be careful to use aseptic technique when we insert the catheter to reduce the risk of infection.

Mrs Kastel: Oh. OK. So, er, you put the tube in and blow that little balloon up so the catheter doesn't fall out, and you have to take care how you put the tube in so I don't get an infection.

Jo: That's exactly it. It's called aseptic technique because it keeps equipment sterile to avoid contamination. The catheter bag you're talking about is one of these. It's a transparent bag which collects the urine that drains out of the catheter. We empty the drainage bag three times a day.

Mrs Kastel: OK, well I hope I won't need it for too long.

Jo: Oh, you shouldn't need it for too long at all.

▬ 6.1

Natasha: Trish, have you got a minute? I just need a drug check. I've got to give Mr Song some morphine.

Trish: Oh sorry, Natasha, I can't at the moment. I'm just in the middle of something, and I can't leave it.

Natasha: No problem. I'll see if Marek's available. Um, do you know where he is?

Trish: Um, I think I saw him in the first bay a little while ago.

Natasha: OK, thanks. I'll see if he's available. Excuse me, Marek.

Marek: Yes?

Natasha: Are you busy at the moment or can you do a drug check with me?

Marek: Sorry, Natasha. I'm tied up at the moment. They've just rung from Theatres. They want Mr Hubble prepped straight away. Can anyone else do it? I've got to do this pre-op check right now.

Natasha: That's OK. I'll have to ask Anna. She should be free. Hi, Anna. Are you free at the moment?

Anna: I will be in a minute. I've just finished this dressing. Just let me just clear the dressing trolley first.

Natasha: Great. Would you mind checking this morphine with me, please?

Anna: Yes, sure. Let me just wash my hands and I'll be with you. Er, who's it for?

▬ 6.2

Natasha: Here's the Medication Chart. It's for Mr Song in bed 16. There we are: Laurence Song, and he's ordered pethidine 100mg IM four hourly.

Anna: Right, yeah, I can see that. Um, Laurence Song, pethidine 100mg IM four hourly. When did he have his last injection?

Natasha: He had it at eleven fifteen this morning, and it's, er, three thirty now, so that's at least four hours in between doses.

Anna: Uh-huh.

Natasha: I've written up the drug book so it's ready for us to sign. Do you mind getting the pethidine from the cupboard? You've got the keys, haven't you?

Anna: Yeah, that's OK. I've got the drug keys on me. OK, pethidine 100mg amps. Here they are. I'll just count them. That's five, ten, fifteen, sixteen, seventeen. I'll take one out for Mr Song and that means there are sixteen left.

Natasha: Sixteen. That's right. I'll sign for it in the book. Can you witness it for me, please?

Anna: Sure. Um ... OK, there's my signature.

Natasha: Great. Here's the amp – pethidine 100mg. I'll just show you the expiry date ... expires oh four two thousand and ten. So it's still OK. Can you see that expiry date?

Anna: I'll have a look. Pethidine 100mg, OK. Expires, um, oh four two thousand and ten. Looks good.

Natasha: Right, now where's the syringe? Here we are. I'll just draw up the amp so you can see it. There it is: two mils. Can you check that for me, please?

Anna: Yes, that looks like two mils.

Natasha: Good, that's done. Thanks, Anna. Can you come with me now and watch me give the injection to Mr Song? I know he's been waiting for it.

■ 6.3

Josh: Susanna, are you busy at the moment? Would you mind checking a medication with me?

Susanna: Sure, just let me put this chart back, and I'll be with you. OK. I'm ready.

Josh: Right. It's for Chris Multer in bed 1. Here's his Medication Chart.

Susanna: Let me see. Chris Multer, yeah, and bed 1, yeah. What's the medication you need checked?

Josh: I need you to check his anticoagulant medication. He's on warfarin at the moment.

Susanna: Mm, warfarin. Yeah, that's what's written here.

Josh: And he's taking it orally.

Susanna: Per oral, yes, that's correct. What time is it due?

Josh: It's due at sixteen hundred hours, so that's now.

Susanna: Sixteen hundred hours. Correct. We just need to check his INR before we give it, don't we? What was his INR result today?

Josh: His INR's down to one point five. Ideally, the doctors want it to be between two and two point five. Until it gets up to that level, he'll be taking 5mg of warfarin; then it can be reduced.

Susanna: Yeah, poor guy. He's been really sick, hasn't he?

Josh: Yeah, he has. All right, here's the bottle of warfarin 5mg. Can you see the label OK to check the dose?

Susanna: Yeah, I can. Um, it's warfarin 5mg.

Josh: I'm taking out one tablet.

Susanna: Yep, one tablet.

Josh: I'll sign the medication chart first. There we are.

Susanna: OK, let me countersign for you. Right, that's done.

Josh: Thanks. I'll go and give it to him now. Thanks for the help.

■ 6.4

Helen: Hello, Mr Albiston. How are you doing?

Mr Albiston: Not too bad, Helen. They started me on a new tablet, I think.

Helen: That's right. The doctor's started you on atorvastatin, so I thought I'd have a chat with you, as there are a few things you need to know about it.

Mr Albiston: OK. What do I have to know?

Helen: The medication is used to prevent atherosclerosis, or clogging of the arteries with fatty deposits.

Mr Albiston: I understand.

Helen: You take the medication once a day as a tablet.

Mr Albiston: Oh, right. Does it take long to work?

Helen: No, it works quite quickly. I've brought a diagram to help you understand what happens when you take this medication. After you swallow the tablet it enters the gastrointestinal tract, or GIT. It passes through the oesophagus. That's this tube here.

Mr Albiston: Mm, the tube which leads to your stomach.

Helen: That's right. The tablet passes into your stomach here, where it's absorbed. It mixes with the liquids there so it can pass into your bloodstream. It then goes into the liver via the small intestine.

Mr Albiston: That's this part under the stomach, isn't it? And it goes across to the liver over here?

Helen: Yes. The drug is metabolised, or chemically changed, in the liver. The liver stops the production of an enzyme which causes the body to produce a harmful type of cholesterol. By inhibiting this enzyme, the amount of 'bad cholesterol' which is released into the blood is reduced. Atorvastatin also increases the amount of a type of 'good cholesterol' in your blood. This is a protective form of cholesterol.

Mr Albiston: I see. So that's why the doctor asked me if I had any problems with my liver. The liver is obviously very important in all this.

Helen: Yes, it is. It's important to check if you have any liver problems before prescribing the medication for you.

Mr Albiston: Yeah, I understand. Is it better to take it at night or in the morning?

Helen: Take it in the morning, because it's absorbed better in the morning than in the evening.

Mr Albiston: OK, I'll remember that.

Helen: I'd also like to talk to you about some precautions you need to take when you're taking this medication at home.

■ 6.5

Sonia: Helen, I wanted to talk to you about Mr Albiston's chart if you don't mind. He's just started atorvastatin, hasn't he?

Helen: Yes. A couple of days ago. I had a talk to him about some things he'll need to be careful of at home.

Sonia: I can see on his chart when he started atorvastatin. I'm a bit concerned about something he was started on today. I noticed that he was put on a multi B vitamin tablet.

Helen: Yeah, right. I noticed that, too. He shouldn't be taking that with atorvastatin. I didn't give it to him. Er, you can see I documented it in his notes.

Sonia: That's good. He shouldn't take Vitamin B3 – I mean, nicotinic acid – on its own or in any other preparation.

Helen: Right, I'll ask the SHO to cancel the order for the multivitamin tablet.

Sonia: That'd be great. Does he know not to drink grapefruit juice with the atorvastatin?

Helen: Oh, yes. I explained all that to him before.

■ 6.6

Jo: Um, Beatriz, are you ready for me to go through this medication assessment with you?

Beatriz: Uh, huh.

Jo: All right, here we are. Hello, Mrs Gilbert. Do you mind if Beatriz gives you your medication as an assessment?

Mrs Gilbert: No, dear, I don't mind at all.

Beatriz: Thanks, Mrs Gilbert. OK. I'm going to follow the 'five rights' of medication administration for patient safety. Mrs Gilbert is ordered Lasix. Erm, it's in her drawer here as furosemide.

Jo: Yes, that's the correct drug, but it should have been ordered by its generic name, furosemide, not its brand, or proprietary, name, Lasix.

Beatriz: Yes, it can be unclear sometimes, can't it? Um, the medication is ordered for Mrs Eileen Gilbert. I'll just check the hospital label on the chart. Mrs Eileen Gilbert, so that's right. If you don't mind, Mrs Gilbert, I'd like to check your identity bracelet, too.

Mrs Gilbert: Why would you do that? You know who I am.

Beatriz: You'd be surprised, Mrs Gilbert. Sometimes two patients with the same name are in the hospital at the same time.

Mrs Gilbert: Oh, fancy that!

Jo: What route of administration do you have to use?

Beatriz: Oral, I suppose. The doctor hasn't written that in.

Jo: That's a problem, isn't it? The doctor may want to use the oral route or IV route.

Beatriz: Ah, I see what you mean.

Jo: What about the dose?

Beatriz: It's not written in. It's usually 40mg, but the dose would depend on her blood levels.

Jo: Quite right. You couldn't assume. It could have dangerous consequences.

Beatriz: Mm. There's a problem with the frequency and time of administration as well. The doctor hasn't noted down the frequency the medication is to be given or the times. That's a problem, especially with furosemide. It's usually given before midday in divided doses so the patient is not troubled by getting up frequently to go to the toilet in the evening.

Jo: Well done. Now, tell me. Would you be happy to give this medication?

■ 7.1

Dr Venturi: Hello, Paula. Are you looking after Mrs Boland today?

Paula: No, that's Suzy, but she's just gone down to X-ray with a patient.

Dr Venturi: Oh, I wanted to review Mrs Boland's IV fluids.

Paula: I'm looking after Suzy's patients while she's away. Do you want me to pass on any updates?

Dr Venturi: Yeah, thanks. Could you take down Mrs Boland's IV when it's finished, please?

Paula: Sure. I'll just write a note about it for Suzy. What about the cannula? Do you want it left in?

Dr Venturi: I think so. Leave it for another day in case she needs some more fluids.

Paula: OK. Do you want to see Mrs Dillip in the next room, too?

Dr Venturi: Yes, I need to see her. According to her blood results her potassium levels are quite low. I'll put in a cannula when I finish my rounds. Could you start her on a litre of Normal Saline with 40 millimols of KCl?

Paula: OK. Here's the Prescription Chart for you to fill out.

Dr Venturi: Thanks. That saves me a bit of leg work. Can you run it over eight hours, please?

Paula: Sure. One litre of Normal Saline with 40 millimols KCl over eight hours.

Dr Venturi: Oh, I'll have to order her some IV antibiotics, too.

Paula: Yeah, OK. We'll run them through a secondary line. The primary line will have the KCl running through, so we won't mix the solutions in the same line.

Dr Venturi: Great. Now there's just Mr Claussen left. How is he?

Paula: He's one of Suzy's patients, too. He's pretty good. He's going home today, I think.

Dr Venturi: Yes, that's right. He's ready for discharge. Can you take out his cannula before he goes home, please?

Paula: Yes, sure, we can do that. I'll pass on your instructions to Suzy when she gets back.

▬ 7.2

Suzy: Hi.

Paula: Hi, Suzy. You're back. Dr Venturi saw some of your patients while you were at X-ray. Mrs Boland first.

Suzy: Oh, OK. What are we doing with her IV?

Paula: He asked if you could take the IV down when it's run through. It's just about through now.

Suzy: Thanks. I'll take it down in a minute. Um. What about the cannula? Does he want it left in or taken out?

Paula: He said to leave the IV cannula in for another day just in case she needs more fluids.

Suzy: Oh, all right. Um, and what about Mrs Dillip? Did he see her, too?

Paula: Yeah. She's quite dehydrated, isn't she?

Suzy: Yeah. And her potassium levels were pretty low, too.

Paula: He asked if you could put up a bag of Normal Saline with 40 millimols of KCl. He just put in a cannula for her.

Suzy: OK. Can you check it out with me and I'll put it up straight away.

Paula: Yeah, I'm free at the moment. I'll check it with you.

Suzy: How long does he want it to run over?

Paula: Let me look at the order. Um ... he wants it to run over eight hours.

Suzy: OK. I'll get the infusion pump and set it up.

Paula: Oh, and he's also ordered some IV antibiotics for her.

Suzy: Oh, right. I'll run them through a secondary line. I don't want to run them through the primary line while she's got KCl running through it.

Paula: Yeah, right. He also saw Mr Claussen. You're looking after him, aren't you?

Suzy: Yes, he's my patient. Any new orders there?

Paula: Only that he said that Mr Claussen's IV cannula could be taken out.

Suzy: Oh.

Paula: He's just finished his course of antibiotics so he doesn't need it in any more. I took it out for him and put on a light dressing because he's going home this afternoon.

Suzy: Oh, thanks.

▬ 7.3

Angela: Hello, Mrs Boxmeer. Can I just check that your IV cannula is all right before I put up the next infusion?

Mrs Boxmeer: Oh, thanks. I was just going to buzz you. The cannula hurts a lot and the IV's not dripping any more.

Angela: OK, it sounds like it might have tissued. It's when the fluid leaks into the tissues and doesn't drip into the vein. I'd also like to check why it's hurting. Can I have a look? Hm, it's quite warm, isn't it?

Mrs Boxmeer: Yes, and it looks red, too.

Angela: So you've got warmth, erythema – that's the redness – and tenderness.

Mrs Boxmeer: Yes, it started being sore a little while ago.

Angela: Sounds like an infection. I'll have a look on your Care Plan to see when the doctor put the IV in. Hm ... three days ago. OK, well it'll need to be resited anyway.

Mrs Boxmeer: What do you mean?

Angela: It means that I'll call the doctor to come and put in a new one. I'll stop this drip now and take out your cannula.

Mrs Boxmeer: I thought that's what you'd have to do. Why do I still have to have one? Can't they leave the cannula out?

Angela: Sorry, you've still got six doses of IV antibiotics so we need to put in a new line.

Mrs Boxmeer: Right, OK. I hope they can find a more convenient spot to put it in.

Angela: I know it was a nuisance, and it was positional, too. Every time you lifted your arm the infusion stopped. The thing is that there is a lower risk of phlebitis if we put the cannula in your hand.

Mrs Boxmeer: Phlebitis? Is that infection?

Angela: Yes. It means inflammation of the vein. More often than not it's caused by a nosocomial infection of staph, or staphylococci bacteria. Staph is usually found on the hands. The best way to prevent infection entering is for health workers to wash their hands properly before touching the cannula site and to use aseptic technique when putting in a new cannula.

Mrs Boxmeer: I see.

Angela: That's why we check the cannula site and take the cannula out at the first sign of infection. Our hospital follows Evidence-Based Practice guidelines which suggest that we take IV cannulas out after seventy-two hours and that we change IV giving sets at the same time as well. The number of days the IV is kept in is recorded in the Care Plan.

▬ 7.4

Kasia: Good morning, Ward 7 West, Kasia speaking.

Dr Gonzalez: Hello, it's Dr Gonzalez here. I'm the Surgical Registrar. I was bleeped about resiting an IV cannula.

Kasia: I'm sorry, I didn't hear your name properly. Who's calling, please?

Dr Gonzalez: It's Dr Gonzalez ... Claudia Gonzalez. I'm the Surgical Registrar for your ward. I was bleeped about resiting a cannula for Mrs Szubansky. Can I please speak to the nurse looking after Mrs Szubansky?

Kasia: Sorry, um, I didn't catch the patient's name. Could you spell it for me, please?

Dr Gonzalez: Yes, it's S-z-u-b-a-n-s-k-y. Do you know who's looking after her?

Kasia: Oh, I know who you mean now. OK, so you need to talk to Mrs Szubansky's nurse about resiting a cannula. Um ... Michael's looking after Mrs Szubansky today. He's just on a break. Can I take a message for him?

Dr Gonzalez: Yeah, look, I'm pretty busy at the moment. I've got a few blood tests to do, but I just wanted to check how urgent the call was.

Kasia: Sorry, Dr Gonzalez. Er, would you mind slowing down a bit? Um, I'm afraid I've missed some of the message.

Dr Gonzalez: Right ... sorry. Could you please ask Michael to call me and let me know how quickly the cannula needs to be resited ... um, let me know when Mrs Szubansky's next IV antibiotics are due.

Kasia: OK, let me just read that message back to you. You want Michael to call and tell you when the cannula needs to be resited and when the next IV antibiotics are due?

Dr Gonzalez: That's right.

Kasia: OK. I'll make sure I pass your message on to Michael. He'll be back from his break in about five minutes or so. Er, can I get a contact number so Michael can return your call?

Dr Gonzalez: Sure, my bleeper number is 645. Thanks, Kasia.

Kasia: You're welcome.

▬ 7.5

Cheryl: Karen, I'm just off to lunch. Do you mind keeping an eye on Miss Hadfield's fluids?

Karen: Sure, no problem. When did she have the IV put in?

Cheryl: On admission yesterday. It was just to KVO while she was having her IV antibiotics, but she became dehydrated and still isn't drinking much. That's why they had to increase her fluids.

Karen: She was in a bad way when she came in, wasn't she? What's up now?

Cheryl: She's got an eight hourly litre of Normal Saline up, but it's just through. Do you mind checking out another bag with me? I can go to lunch then.

Karen: Sure. Have you got the Prescription Chart with you?

Cheryl: Yeah, here it is. Here's her hospital label ... Mabyn Hadfield ... unit number 62388 ... date of birth 12th January, 1920.

Karen: OK. Normal Saline – that's the litre up now?

Cheryl: That's right. One litre of Normal Saline over eight hours. It went up at 03.00 hours and it's through now at 11.00 hours so I'll write that in here. And I'll write in the amount of a thousand mils. There. Now we can check out the next one. The date is 30th of May, the route is IV and the fluid is five per cent Dextrose.

Karen: 30th, yes, IV, yes, five per cent Dextrose, yes.

Cheryl: OK. We can check the IV infusion now. Here's the bag. I'll just show you. Five per cent Dextrose. It expires on the 16th of July 2010. Can you see the expiry date on the bag OK?

Karen: Yeah. Five per cent Dextrose, expires 16th of July 2010. Correct.

Cheryl: Right, so let me write it in. 30th May, 11.00 hours. The rate is one litre over ten hours. That's easy to work out. One litre – a thousand mils – divided by ten hours. That's a hundred mils an hour.

Karen: Looks good.

Cheryl: OK. My initial here under Nurse one. CA.

Karen: And my initial here under Nurse two. KB.

Cheryl: Thanks. Do you mind putting it up so I can have my break now?

Karen: No, go ahead. I'll put it up for you.

Cheryl: Thanks.

▬▬ 7.6

Rebecca: Look at this Fluid Balance Chart, Casey. It's a mess!

Casey: I see what you mean. Whose is it?

Rebecca: It's Miss Stavel's. You remember, she's the one who lost a lot of blood during her operation.

Casey: Yes, I remember. What's her oral intake like?

Rebecca: It's hard to tell. There's no record of any intake from 10 am to 5 pm. I don't know if she drank anything at all. And at 5 pm they recorded the amount of water she drank inaccurately. It was recorded as 'half a cup'. It's impossible to know what size cup!

Casey: Right. I wonder if they explained how the chart worked to her before they started it. Otherwise you can't expect her to comply at all.

Rebecca: I'm not sure.

Casey: What about her IV intake?

Rebecca: Her IV intake's been recorded accurately. She's had a few litres today. They did record the extra fluid given with IV antibiotics correctly.

Casey: What about her output? What's that like?

Rebecca: She's been vomiting a lot, as you can see, but they haven't been able to measure it properly every time.

Casey: It's hard to know what 'large amount' or 'small amount' means, isn't it?

Rebecca: Mm, yes. There's also a problem with the record of her urine output. She's obviously been incontinent – there are a few 'wet beds' recorded. See here at 4 am wet bed one plus and at 8 am she had a wet bed two pluses. They can't have been able to measure her urine output with any accuracy.

Casey: And according to the chart she hasn't passed urine since lunchtime. That can't be right. It says here she was 'up to the toilet' at 1 pm. It really doesn't look as though it was explained to her at all. At least she's not showing any signs of urinary retention and she's not uncomfortable.

Rebecca: And the drains were emptied and recorded.

Casey: Well, there's no point adding up the intake and output because of the mistakes so it won't be much use for assessing her fluid status.

Rebecca: No, it doesn't look like it. They'll have to rely on her daily weight.

Casey: Let me see her Obs. Chart. Ah, yes. They have weighed her daily, so that's good.

▬▬ 8.1

Alexandra: Hello, Mrs Clarke. I'm Alexandra. I'll be looking after you today. Have you settled in yet?

Mrs Clarke: Yes, dear. I've met all the ladies in my room. I just have to wait for the operation now, don't I?

Alexandra: Yes. I'm going to look at the operation list when it comes out later today so I can tell you where you are on the list. I just need to go through some pre-op things with you. Is that okay?

Mrs Clarke: Yes, that's fine. Um, I've brought my letter from the doctor for you. Here it is.

Alexandra: Thanks, Mrs Clarke. Right, let me see. First, I'll check your consent form. Is that your signature?

Mrs Clarke: Yes, dear. I signed it in the doctor's surgery before I came to the hospital. He explained all about the operation to me.

Alexandra: Good. Now, I'll get you to take off your nail polish later today so the anaesthetist will be able to see your nail beds.

Mrs Clarke: Oh.

Alexandra: And you'll also need to shower with this antiseptic wash. Here's a sachet of the wash for you. Just wash all over using the antiseptic wash as you would with soap.

Mrs Clarke: All right. I'll do that tonight before I go to bed.

Alexandra: Great. I'll get you to have another shower with the antiseptic wash in the morning. I'll give you another sachet in a while.

Mrs Clarke: Will my tummy be shaved before the operation?

Alexandra: No, it won't. We used to shave the operation area but the policy has changed now.

Mrs Clarke: Oh.

Alexandra: Best practice is that if it doesn't interfere with the surgery, then the area is not shaved.

Mrs Clarke: Oh good. I remember having it done many years ago when I had an operation. It wasn't very comfortable.

Alexandra: I know what you mean. A lot of people used to complain about it. Now, I see that you've been on a low-residue diet for a

few days. I'm going to order you clear fluids for today. That means you'll just be on liquids today. Then you'll be Nil By Mouth after midnight. I've got the Nil By Mouth sign here which I'll put up a little later. It just reminds the kitchen staff not to leave you a meal.

Mrs Clarke: Oh yes. That means I won't be able to eat or drink anything after midnight, will I?

Alexandra: No, you won't. The reason for this is that when you have an anaesthetic, your muscles relax. If you have anything in your stomach it could rise up into your throat and you might inhale it.

Mrs Clarke: Oh, I see. I certainly don't want that to happen.

Alexandra: No, not at all. I'll get you to take a special bowel preparation drink later to clean out your bowel. You'll also need a small enema to help you to open your bowels. This is so that when the surgeon operates, there is less chance of contamination from the bowel contents.

Mrs Clarke: It's quite a business, isn't it?

Alexandra: Yes, it does take a bit of preparation. Oh, I'm going to do one last thing.

Mrs Clarke: I hope it won't taste awful.

Alexandra: [*laughs*] No, it's not anything like that. I'm gonna to get you some anti-embolic stockings. They're very firm stockings; you put them on to support your legs. You wear them to prevent deep vein thrombosis – DVTs – or clots in your veins.

Mrs Clarke: That's all right then. They won't be too much of a bother, I'm sure.

▬▬ 8.2

Alva: Hello, I'm Alva. I'll be looking after you today, er, Ms Slade. Do you mind if I call you by your first name?

Emma: No. Hi, Alva. Nice to meet you. Please call me Emma.

Alva: OK, thanks. I always like to ask first. Um, I wanted to have a talk to you about your operation tomorrow.

Emma: Oh. Is everything all right? There's nothing wrong, is there?

Alva: No, no, not at all, everything's fine. I'll just bring this chair up so I can sit with you. Um, there are no problems. I just want to go through what will happen when you come back to the ward after the operation. People always feel better when they know what to expect.

Emma: Oh, yes, you're right. I'm so nervous about the operation. I haven't been in a hospital since I was a kid, when I broke my leg. Things have probably changed since then.

Alva: Well, hospitals have changed a bit, but don't worry, I'll go through it all now, and you'll have the opportunity to ask as many questions as you like.

Emma: Thanks. I feel silly being so worried. I'm not normally like this.

Alva: That's OK, Emma. It's quite normal to feel a bit apprehensive. Um, I'll try and cover everything so you're prepared for what'll happen after the operation. Um, I see you've brought the leaflet about keyhole surgery.

Emma: Yes, um, it was sent to me at home last week. The only thing I know is that I won't have a big cut so the operation won't leave a big scar. I'll just have a couple of small holes in my tummy.

Alva: That's right. Um, keyhole surgery is also called minimally invasive surgery because it's performed with the use of a laparoscope, using small incisions or surgical cuts. Um, you'll probably have three to four puncture sites. These are just small holes made near your navel. And you'll have a small dressing covering the holes made during surgery. It's just a light covering to keep the area clean until it heals.

Emma: Oh.

Alva: During the operation, the surgeon uses a laparoscope, which is passed through the holes to visualise your gallbladder. The infected gallbladder is removed through the largest puncture site. You'll have a mini-drain which will only stay in for a couple of hours. It's a small plastic container attached to some tubing which takes away any excess blood from your wound.

Emma: Ah-hah. There won't be lots of blood, will there? I can't stand the sight of blood.

Alva: No, not much, but I can make a note for the rest of the staff to cover the drain for you so you don't see any of it.

Emma: Thanks. Um, will I have a drip in my arm?

Alva: Yes, you will. You'll come back with an IV and some fluids running, just until you can eat and drink again.

Emma: Will I be able to eat straight away?

Alva: You'll have had a tube down your throat for the anaesthetic, so we'll need to make sure that your swallow reflex is working again after the tube's been removed. We check that you can swallow again by trying you with a few ice chips. As soon as you can manage the ice chips, we'll give you small sips of water. Um, we'll also need to be sure that your bowels are working again before you try eating small amounts of food.

Emma: Oh, is that why they do that? I never knew. It makes sense to go slowly.

Alva: The other tube you'll have is an indwelling catheter, which they'll put in while you are in Theatres. Um, it can be taken out when you're back on the ward and think you can void again – um, I mean, pass urine. Um, you won't have the catheter for too long. Now, I'm just going to get something to show you so I can go through the rest of the information.

8.3

Alva: OK, Emma, er, can I go through the rest of this post-op information with you now?

Emma: Er, yeah, thanks. Actually, there's something that concerns me a lot. Um, what about pain? I'm worried that I'll be in a lot of pain.

Alva: You'll have a PCA machine to use for any discomfort after the operation. That's what I wanted to show you, so I've brought one along for you to see what it's like. It's patient-controlled analgesia which will be run through an IV line and a pump. The medication goes into your bloodstream whenever you push this button.

Emma: Oh. Er, so I won't be in pain. I was really worried about that. But what if I keep pushing the button? Won't I give myself an overdose?

Alva: No, don't worry. We program the pump so there's a lock-out time. Even if you keep pushing the button, no more medication will go through the line.

Emma: Ah, right.

Alva: The machine automatically blocks it, or locks it out. Um, the nurses will be taking your obs. – I mean, your observations – like your temperature, pulse and blood pressure. They'll also check your pain level. Erm, they'll check all these frequently, so they'll keep a good eye on you.

Emma: That's a relief. I think the fear of being in pain was making me unable to cope with the idea of surgery. Is there anything else that I'll have to do after the operation?

Alva: Just two more things. I see the physio has given you an incentive spirometer, er, a tri-ball, to blow into.

Emma: Yeah.

Alva: You'll have to use the tri-ball every hour that you are awake.

Emma: Yes, she's had me practising every hour. I've been trying to blow harder each time but it's quite difficult.

Alva: Yes, it is quite hard. Um, the physio would have told you how important it is to use this to prevent lung collapse, by making sure your lungs inflate as much as possible.

Emma: Yes, she did. Um, I understand it's to get your lung function back after the anaesthetic.

8.4

Nasreen: Hello, Mr Vitellis. How are you doing? Everything all right?

Mr Vitellis: Yes, thanks, Nasreen. I'm fine. I was just wondering if you could explain what's happening about this clot in my leg.

Nasreen: Oh, sure. I can explain it to you. I'll get you one of the ward brochures which help explain it very well. Just a minute. Starting with the first picture, this shows normal blood flow as it moves smoothly through your arteries and veins. Strong muscles surround the deep veins and help to pump the blood back to the lungs where the blood is oxygenated again.

Mr Vitellis: I see. So why does a clot form? Does something happen to the blood flow? The doctors explained that lying flat for a long time doesn't help blood flow much.

Nasreen: Yes, that's right. Orthopaedic operations take a long time and so patients lie flat on the operating table for several hours. This gives them a higher risk of getting a DVT than patients undergoing operations which last a shorter time. In surgical cases there are three factors which contribute to the risk of DVT occurring during or just after surgery. The first factor is caused by patients lying without moving on the operating table. Because the body is immobile for so long, blood flow is slowed and the blood doesn't return to the heart as efficiently as usual. Blood starts to pool, or collect, in the lower legs. This pooling of the blood in the veins is called venous stasis.

Mr Vitellis: I see.

Nasreen: The second factor is a result of the venous stasis. As the blood flow slows, the veins stretch. This is called venodilation. The stretching of the veins causes damage to the inner wall of the veins. Gradually, small tears appear.

Mr Vitellis: Oh, I didn't know that.

Nasreen: Mm, the tears in the vessel walls activate a clotting response to the tissue injury.

That's the third factor. As the blood slows, it becomes stickier and blood clots form quite easily in the lower legs.

Mr Vitellis: Is that why my lower leg started to hurt?

Nasreen: Yes, calf pain is one of the signs of a DVT. The other signs are warmth and swelling.

Mr Vitellis: Mm, it certainly is painful; it's still quite warm, too.

Nasreen: Mm, look at the picture in the middle of the diagram: it shows a blood clot forming in a deep vein. And if you have a look at the last picture, you'll understand why you've already started taking anticoagulant medication. That's medication which stops any more clots from forming.

Mr Vitellis: Oh, so the last picture's not a DVT?

Nasreen: No, it shows what happens if the DVT is not treated. Around seven to ten days after the original thrombus, or clot, has formed, a piece of the clot can break off and be carried along in the blood vessel. A blood clot which breaks off is then called an embolus.

Mr Vitellis: Yeah, yeah, I've read a bit about them. They're dangerous, aren't they?

Nasreen: Yes, they are dangerous when they get stuck in blood vessels and block the blood circulation. The condition is called an embolism. The type of embolism which is most dangerous is a pulmonary embolism, because it can block the blood flow to the lungs.

Mr Vitellis: I can see why my DVT is being treated fairly aggressively.

Nasreen: Yes. I've taken the anti-embolic stocking off the leg with the DVT but you still need to keep a stocking on the other leg. I'll come back in a little while and talk to you about the medication you'll be taking.

Mr Vitellis: Thanks. Yeah, I'd like to understand about that, too.

8.5

Viki: Hello, Belinda. Er, they've just called from Theatres and asked me to prep you. I'll just go through this checklist with you, and then I'll give you a pre-med to relax you a bit, OK? Feeling all right?

Belinda: Yes, I think I'm OK. The evening nurse went through everything about the operation with me last night so I know what to expect.

Viki: Good. Now, first of all I'm going to verify who you are, including your hospital number. You'll be asked the same information by lots of people along the way. Don't worry, it's just our checking system. Ah, now, can you tell me your full name, please?

Belinda: Sure. Belinda Anne Mainwaring.

Viki: Can I check your identity bracelets, too, please?

Belinda: Yes, here they are. I've got two on.

Viki: Thanks, Belinda. That's six seven nine oh three, er, correct on both of them. Can you tell me what operation you're going to have?

Belinda: Oh, um, they're going to fix the tendon in my right shoulder.

Viki: Right, so that's a right shoulder arthroscopy for a rotator cuff repair. Er, great. Have you signed a consent form for the operation?

Belinda: Yes, I signed it yesterday.

Viki: I'll just show you this signature. Is this your signature?

Belinda: Er, yes, that's my signature.

Viki: OK, now did the surgeon come up and mark the operation site?

Belinda: Yes, look, I've got pen marks on my right shoulder.

Viki: Yes, you have. Er, right, now I've got all your charts together – um, Drug Chart, Prescription Chart for IV fluids, Patient Record and Fluid Balance Chart. So, I'll tick that section. Um, have you had any X-rays done in hospital?

Belinda: Yes, I had an X-ray when I first came in.

Viki: Right, I'll get them and add them to your chart, which we'll take down to Theatres. Do you have any allergies?

Belinda: Er, no, not that I know of.

Viki: OK, that's a 'No' for allergies. And, er, I'll circle 'No' next to 'Red bracelet worn' as you don't need one. Now, on to your teeth. Do you have any caps on your teeth, or crowns, or bridges?

Belinda: No, I don't.

Viki: OK. I can write 'No' for that, too. You don't have dentures either, do you?

Belinda: No, all my own teeth.

Viki: Yeah, I thought so, but we have to ask to be sure. The operation site wasn't shaved, was it?

Belinda: No, the surgeon just came and marked the operation area.

Viki: Right. Er, have you taken off your nail varnish?

Belinda: Yes, er, I did that this morning. Why do you have to take it off?

Viki: It's to minimise infection and also to make it easier to check your circulation while you're under anaesthetic. Um, I need you to take off any jewellery you have. Metal is also a safety risk in Theatres.

Belinda: Oh, I didn't bring any jewellery to the hospital, but I don't really want to take my wedding ring off.

Viki: That's all right. I'll just tape it on securely so the metal is covered.

Belinda: Thanks.

Viki: OK. Next question. Do you have any piercings?

Belinda: No, I don't.

Viki: Right, so that's also 'N/A' for piercings – it's not applicable to you. I've nearly finished the questions. How are you doing? Can I keep going?

Belinda: Yes, I'm OK. I feel quite relaxed.

Viki: Right, I can see you've got a theatre gown on. Have you got your anti-embolic stockings on?

Belinda: Yes, here they are, on nice and smoothly as you showed me. I've even put on the disposable knickers you left me.

Viki: Good work. Er, ah, when was the last time you passed urine?

Belinda: About five minutes before you came to check me. So, ten twenty I think.

Viki: OK, last void was 10.20 am. Let me see, I need to circle 'N/A' next to catheterised because you don't have a catheter. Now, when was the last time you had something to eat or drink?

Belinda: Er, I had dinner last night at, what, 6 pm, I think, and a last drink of water at 11 pm before the nurse put up the Nil By Mouth sign and took the water jug away.

Viki: That's good. As long as you have the last drink at least six hours before surgery. You don't want to risk vomiting after your surgery. All right, I'm going to give you your pre-med now.

Belinda: Er, pre-med? Does that mean I'm going to sleep now?

Viki: No, it's not an anaesthetic. You'll just feel calm and relaxed.

Belinda: That's good.

Viki: There you are. Now, I'll just sign the Checklist and we'll wait for the porters to take you to Theatres.

▬ 8.6

Wendy: Hello, I'm Wendy. I'm a Theatre Nurse and I'm going to check you in today. How are you doing?

Belinda: All right.

Wendy: That's good. I'm just going to go through this Checklist again. OK? Um, I know you've already answered many of these questions, but we like to double-check everything, OK?

Belinda: Yes, that's fine.

Wendy: Right, can you tell me your full name, please?

Belinda: Yes, Belinda Anne Mainwaring.

Wendy: Thank you. I'll have a quick look at your identification bracelets if I may?

Belinda: Sure, here they are.

Wendy: Belinda Anne Mainwaring, number six seven four nine oh three, correct. Can you tell me what operation you're having today?

Belinda: Yes, I'm having the tendon in my right shoulder repaired.

Wendy: Mm, did you sign a consent form for the operation?

Belinda: Yes, I did.

Wendy: Is this your signature on the consent form?

Belinda: Yes, it is.

Wendy: All right, nearly finished. Have you had a pre-med?

Belinda: Yes, I had an injection just before I came here.

Wendy: Mm, pre-med given and signed for. Great. All right, I'll sign the Checklist and you've already got a theatre cap to cover your hair. You'll be waiting here for a few more minutes and then we'll take you through. Are you all right there?

Belinda: Yes, thanks.

▬ 9.1

Hazel: Hello, I've got Roli Davidson back from Theatres. Are you taking over his care?

Georgia: Yes, that's me. Hello, Roli, you're back on the ward now from Recovery. Can you hear me?

Roli: Mnnn.

Georgia: I'll just get a quick handover, and then I'll help make you a bit more comfortable. OK?

Roli: Mnnn.

Hazel: OK, Georgia, I'll just go through the operation report with you. Um, Roli Davidson

came in after an RTA, er, he had the motor bike accident this morning.

Georgia: Ah huh.

Hazel: He's had a splenectomy today at 11.15 am. The operation was uneventful. No post-op complications, except a bit of delayed awakening.

Georgia: Mm. He's still a bit drowsy, isn't he?

Hazel: Yes, a bit. I put him on neuro obs. to keep an eye on it. I've put the chart in his notes. His GCS was ten out of fifteen at first. He was opening his eyes to pain, making incomprehensible sounds and obeying commands for movement. When he left Recovery, his GCS was thirteen out of fifteen. He opens his eyes to command. Roli, can you open your eyes for me?

Roli: Urgh.

Hazel: That's it. Do you know where you are, Roli?

Roli: Um, hospital.

Georgia: That's it, you're back on the ward.

Hazel: Right, his obs. are stable, temp thirty-six, pulse seventy-two, BP one twelve over sixty-four, oxygen sats are ninety-seven per cent on three litres of oxygen.

Georgia: I'll just switch over to our oxygen. Roli, I'm changing the oxygen tubing over to our wall unit. Can you just breathe normally for me?

Roli: Mm, yeah. OK

Hazel: That's it. OK, fluids. He's got a litre of five per cent dextrose running.

Georgia: Right. I'll just transfer the bag to our IV stand now. There we are.

Hazel: That litre is due in an hour or so, and there are more fluids written up on the Prescription Chart. Er, Roli had a few episodes of vomiting post-op, so you might like to keep the IV going for a while. He was given an anti-emetic and he has a prn order in case he has any nausea later on.

Georgia: Great. Er, what about drains?

Hazel: He's got one redivac in situ. Roli, can I have a look at your drain for a minute?

Roli: Yeah. OK.

Hazel: Here it is. It's patent. Let's just have a look. Yes, it's working well. And it's draining small amounts. It's to be removed when it drains less than twenty mils a day.

Georgia: OK. OK.

Hazel: Roli, can I check the wound now? I'll just take the blanket off for a minute. There it is. The wound was closed with clips, as you can see. There are just six clips. The wound's been covered with a non-adhesive dressing. Leave it intact until review by the surgeon tomorrow, please.

Georgia: OK. Er, what about analgesia?

Hazel: He's been ordered pethidine seventy-five mg IM three hourly for three days, then oral analgesia. He was given pethidine seventy-five mg just before leaving Recovery at, er, 1.30 pm. I gave him an extra blanket, too, as he was a bit hypothermic.

Georgia: Right. Thanks. Are you feeling warm enough now, Roli?

Roli: Um, yeah, I'm OK now. Just sleepy.

Georgia: All right, I'll just put your notes back, and then I'll come and take a few obs. and make you comfortable.

9.2

Georgia: Hello, Roli. I'll just do some more obs. and see how you're doing.

Roli: OK.

Georgia: OK, temp thirty-six one, pulse sixty-eight, BP a hundred and six over sixty, and your oxygen sats ninety-six per cent on three litres of oxygen. I'll take the oxygen off in a little while, OK? Your temp's still down a bit. Are you warm enough now?

Roli: [incomprehensible]

Georgia: Sorry, Roli. I didn't catch that. I'll just take your mask off for a minute.

Roli: No, not really. Um, I'm still feeling cold. Is that normal?

Georgia: Yeah, it's OK. It's called hypothermia. It happens sometimes if the operation takes a long time. I'll get you an extra blanket to help warm you up. Are you quite awake after the operation?

Roli: Yeah, I'm awake now, um, but I still feel a bit groggy.

Georgia: That's because you've had an anaesthetic. You'll feel better soon.

Roli: I hope so. My throat feels really sore. It's hard to swallow.

Georgia: Don't worry, that's normal. It's just caused by the tube they put down your throat during surgery. I'll get you some ice chips to suck soon.

Roli: Thanks. I don't think I could manage anything else. I feel like I'd be sick if I ate anything.

Georgia: Mm, nausea is sometimes a reaction to post-operative pain. I'll keep an eye on that. How's the pain level now?

Roli: Oh, I'm in bad pain, and everything hurts.

Georgia: That's, that's quite normal. Patients who've had abdominal surgery are often in quite a bit of discomfort. I'll get you an injection for the pain.

Roli: Good, thanks a lot. I feel like I can't move because it's going to be painful.

Georgia: Mm, it's quite common to avoid any movement which might cause discomfort, but it's important that I help you to move around and change position.

Roli: Oh, I can hardly wait for that! It's strange. I feel as if I want to go to the toilet all the time.

Georgia: It's quite usual to have that sensation, even though you've got a catheter in your bladder. Sometimes the catheter needs a little adjustment so it's more comfortable.

Roli: I feel dizzy, too. It's like I'm going to fall out of bed.

Georgia: That's OK. It takes a little while to be orientated again after an anaesthetic. I'm going to put these bed rails up while you're feeling a bit wobbly and get you some pain relief. Here's the call bell if you need me.

Roli: Thanks.

9.3

Patricia: Hello, Paul. How are you feeling now?

Paul: Oh, not too good. Everything hurts.

Patricia: Mm, I can imagine. You've got a lot of cuts and bruises. Can you tell me where the pain is?

Paul: Yeah. My head, my cheek ... um, the broken cheek, I mean. My arms hurt where the cuts are and my chest hurts, too.

Patricia: OK. Can you tell me if the pain is the same all over or different?

Paul: I've got a throbbing headache, and my right cheek hurts when I touch it.

Patricia: That'll be because you've got a broken cheek bone. The pain is referred to your head and you get a headache.

Paul: Oh, OK. That makes sense.

Patricia: What about the pain in your arms and chest?

Paul: It's a stinging pain in the shallow cuts, but this cut in my chest is quite deep, and the pain's like a knife.

Patricia: When's the pain worse, Paul?

Paul: It's worse when I turn over or move.

Patricia: OK, can you rate the pain for me? On a scale of zero to ten, zero is when you feel no pain and ten is when you feel the worst pain that you can imagine. What's the pain like now you are at rest?

Paul: It's around six.

Patricia: And when you move a bit?

Paul: It gets worse. Seven, at least.

Patricia: All right, I'll get you something for the pain. Now, I notice you've been ordered paracetamol four hourly.

Paul: Yeah, I don't want it. It ain't strong enough.

Patricia: No, not on its own, but they order it for you because it works with the opioid painkillers to reduce the amount you need to take.

Paul: Er?

Patricia: I mean, it reduces the number of injections you need to have by twenty to thirty per cent. It's important to keep taking the paracetamol regularly.

Paul: Oh, I see. That's different then.

Patricia: Is there anything else which relieves the pain?

Paul: One of the nurses gave me a heat pack for my chest, and that helped.

Patricia: All right. I'll get the painkillers for you and try and put you in a comfortable position with some more pillows. I'll get a heat pack, too.

Paul: Thanks. I'll try to get some rest. It's hard to sleep when you're in pain.

Patricia: Yes, it is. I'll pull the curtains around and dim the lights a bit for you as well. There you go.

9.4

Patricia: Bev, do you mind if we sit here at the Nurses' Station while I hand over my patients? I just want to keep an eye on Paul Vargas over there. I've been watching him with his visitors, and I think it's a good idea to be close by. They're getting a bit loud by the sound of it. I think it's a good idea to watch the situation in case we have to defuse it and calm things down.

Bev: Oh, that's fine. I noticed a lot of visitors around the bed, and their voices seem to be getting a bit louder, don't they?

Patricia: Mm, yes, they do. Well, let's do this handover while we keep an eye on them. Paul's a 19-year-old who got a fractured zygoma with multiple lacerations on his chest after a drunken brawl after that football match at the weekend.

Bev: Yeah, I remember. A&E was full after the match finished.

Patricia: He's in a lot of pain, and we're giving him regular morphine. He's got a past history of drug abuse. The trouble is that you hear him on the phone to his mates telling them that it's great, he gets the injections every time he wants and he says he's stoned all the time.

Bev: OK. That's difficult, isn't it? I'll keep an eye on it. When did he have his last—

Mark Fellows: Hey you, nurse. Yeah, you. Give Paul his injection now. Can't you see he's in pain? You nurses don't do a bloody thing round here. He's in pain and he's giving me grief about it. I can't do anything about it. It's not my job.

Bev: It's OK, I'll see what I can do. I'll be looking after Paul this evening. Can I ask who you are first, please?

Mark Fellows: I'm Mark Fellows. I'm Paul's uncle. Don't worry about who I am. Do something for him. He's in real pain, and you're just sitting there doing nothing.

Bev: All right, Mr Fellows. I need you to lower your voice so we can talk about sorting out Paul's pain. OK? I can't understand what you're saying if you shout at me.

Mark Fellows: Yeah, OK, OK. Sorry. Look, it's just that he needs something for the pain. You're just sitting there. You know, you could be doing something to help him. Why don't the nurses ever get him anything? He's always complaining he's in pain.

Patricia: I do understand, it's hard, isn't it? You feel very helpless when you see someone in pain and you can't do anything about it yourself.

Mark Fellows: Right.

Patricia: You're worried that Paul isn't getting regular pain relief, is that right?

Mark Fellows: Right.

Patricia: How about if I get his chart now and see what he's been having. I can see if he's due for something now. All right?

Mark Fellows: Yeah, yeah, all right. Look, sorry, sorry, nurse. I shouldn't shout at you. It's just that, well, he lives with me, you know. I'm more like his father. I hate to see him like this.

Patricia: Don't worry, we all have to let off steam sometimes. As I said before, Paul is getting regular pain relief. I'll come and talk to him about talking to his nurse before the pain gets too bad. If he's still in pain after he has an injection, he needs to let us know, and we'll see about having the order reviewed.

Mark Fellows: Can you do that? I mean, I thought he just had to put up with it?

Patricia: No. It's really important that Paul lets us know about these sort of things because we can help before things get out of hand.

Mark Fellows: Oh. OK. I hope you won't take it out on Paul just 'cos I lost it.

Bev: Of course not, Mr Fellows. Being in hospital is very stressful, especially for parents, and it sounds like you're more like a dad to Paul than an uncle. Don't worry, we understand.

9.5

Sonia: Now, post-operative pain is acute pain, and with the correct management should decrease over a few days or so after the operation, depending on the individual patient's pain tolerance. It's important to be clear about pain threshold and pain tolerance. The pain threshold is the point at which we all feel pain, for example the temperature that water reaches when it is felt as burning or scalding pain. Pain tolerance is a more individual sensing of pain and can be affected by several things, like cultural factors for instance. Some patients have a high tolerance for pain and some have a low tolerance for pain.

Nurse 1: This would be why we ask for patients to assess their own pain level on a pain scale. It's quite subjective.

Sonia: Mm, that's right. Now, I'm going to talk about the different analgesics which are used in acute post-operative pain. Analgesics act on different sites of the body and are therefore useful for the various types of post-op pain which we talked about earlier.

Nurse 2: You mean localised and referred pain?

Sonia: Yes. We talked about fast pain which is felt at the site of the surgical incision – that is, localised pain. Anti-inflammatory drugs are useful for this type of pain. Non-steroidals are a good example. However, dull, aching pain which is referred from body organs is best treated with opioids, or morphine-like drugs. Opioids can be used to modify or change the transmission of nerve impulses in the dorsal horn. In this way, the opioids pre-empt painful nerve impulses before they cause discomfort. Opioids are also used because it is thought that they mimic the body's natural painkillers, called endorphins. Endorphins are naturally found in the brain.

Nurse 1: What about paracetamol?

Sonia: Good question. It is sometimes discounted as just a medication for minor ailments, but in fact it's very useful. It's not only used as an anti-pyretic drug, to bring down high temperatures, but also as a background drug to opioids.

Nurse 2: Is that why patients are ordered four hourly paracetamol while their pain is being managed with an opioid?

Sonia: Yes, it is. Using paracetamol with opioids reduces the amount of opioids a patient needs by up to thirty per cent. It's quite important to explain that to them because they often refuse the paracetamol, thinking they don't need it. You can see by the different modes of action of analgesics why pain relief is multimodal. Each drug has a specific job to do. Pain management is about using several drugs together to obtain the best outcome. The aim of managing pain in this way is to limit the need for breakthrough doses of pain relief.

9.6

Sarah: Hello, Sharon. Look, Anton. It's Sharon. She's got that name badge on that you like.

Sharon: Hello, Sarah. I think Anton likes the stickers I give him after his medicine even better, don't you?

Anton: Mm.

Sharon: Ah, still hurts to talk, doesn't it, Anton? I'm going to get you some medicine to help your sore throat, but I want you to tell me first how much it hurts. All right?

Anton: Mm.

Sharon: I'm going to show you my sad and happy faces. They're very useful for kids who can't talk because they've got a sore throat. You just have to point to the face which looks like the way you feel. Is that a good idea?

Anton: Mm, yeah.

Sharon: OK, Anton, here are the faces. Can you see this face here, this first face. Can you see he's smiling?

Anton: Mm.

Sharon: He feels great. Nothing hurts. The next face feels pretty good, but it hurts a little bit. He can put up with it.

Sarah: I see, the faces relate to the pain level.

Sharon: That's right. We like to use the Wong–Baker chart, or faces chart, with our younger patients. Any child from the age of around three can use this chart. It's also useful for patients who can't express themselves well enough in English to explain their pain level. Now then, Anton, if you look at face number three, he's starting to look a bit sad, isn't he? He's got quite a lot of pain. It hurts when he moves about. And look at number four. Can you see that he looks really unhappy? He's got a frown on his face, and he can't concentrate on anything.

Sarah: Look, Anton. He's not very happy at all, is he?

Anton: No.

Sharon: And the next little fellow's feeling worse. The pain's very bad now. He's feeling very bad. This poor guy's crying and can't even get out of bed because it hurts so much. It's the worst pain he's ever felt. Now, Anton, can you help me by pointing to the face which is showing how you feel right now? Does your throat hurt a little bit or a lot?

Anton: Er, it hurts a bit. It hurts like the third one.

Sharon: Oh, face number three. OK, so it hurts quite a bit, but it's not as bad as last night after the operation. All right. I'm going to get you some medicine for the pain now. After you've had the medicine, you might feel like playing one of our video games. What do you think? Playing games always takes your mind off feeling uncomfortable, doesn't it?

Sarah: Thanks, Sharon. I might even be able to pop out for a coffee while Anton's playing.

Sharon: Sure. OK, Anton. I'll get you all comfy with this warm blanket, because being warm helps the pain as well. Er, I'll bring you the medicine, and then I'll get a video game for you to play. We'll let mum go and have a cup of coffee, shall we?

Anton: OK. Do you know the game I want?

Sharon: I think so. I'll get the one you were playing yesterday. OK?

Anton: Great!

10.1

Andrea: Let's start with Lidia. Lidia's an 80-year-old Russian lady who's been living in her own home for 40 years; she's a very independent woman. You might remember that her daughters had visited her on a Sunday morning as usual and found her to be uncoordinated; um, she was having trouble picking up her cup of tea. They noticed that she was slurring her speech as well. Lidia said she'd had a 'funny turn' the night before so, unfortunately, by the time they brought her to hospital it was well over the initial three hours from the onset of the stroke. She's been with us for two weeks now and has been working really hard with everyone so that she can get back to her own home. The purpose of this meeting is for us to report back on what we've all been doing for Lidia. Then we need to finalise her discharge plan. William, do you want to kick off?

William: Mm, I examined her yesterday, and I feel that she's doing well, medically. I've spoken to Lidia, and she seems keen to go home. She struck me as a very independent person, too. I asked her about her goals and going home seems to be top of the list.

Andrea: Yes, she's spoken to me about how she was managing at home before the stroke. Her daughters are very supportive, too, which will be good. She'll need a lot of help with her ADLs. Kim, how did you find her?

Kim: I agree with both of you. She's been trying really hard. She's been doing all the physio exercises I give her. It's just … I'm a little concerned about her ability to perform the basic ADLs, especially showering, toileting, eating and mobility.

William: Yes, I'm a bit worried about that as well. Um, why don't we have a look at the home assessment? Has the Occupational Therapist team done a home assessment yet?

Andrea: Not yet. I've booked a home assessment with Occupational Therapy on Monday, 12th June. That'll give us a better idea about the sort of adaptions which need to be made for safety and to allow her to be as independent as possible.

Kim: Good. I'm pleased with her progress. The weakness on her left side has partially resolved. Unfortunately, she's still got a bit of trouble with vision loss on that side. I've been training her to turn to the left to look for anything she might run into.

Andrea: Um, Lidia's going to stay with her daughter, Larissa, until the safety modifications in the house are finished.

William: That's good. Tina, what about speech and language therapy? How's she doing?

Tina: OK, well my role has been to help Lidia's swallow reflex. I've been concentrating on her swallowing problem and speech difficulties. Remember she had quite a lot of difficulty swallowing when she first came in.

Andrea: Yes, her nutritional status was quite poor. There was also the cultural aspect, too. She wasn't used to the food they serve in hospital.

Tina: No, it's very different from her usual diet. Her daughters helped out with this one. They've been bringing in the food which she likes. The kitchen staff have puréed it for her. She still has some tongue and lip weakness. It's quite hard for her to speak properly. I've been practising a lot of mouth exercises with her, and she's certainly improving. She's always been a very social person, according to her daughters, so the ability to communicate is important to her.

William: Have you referred her for speech and language therapy after discharge?

Tina: No, I haven't referred her to a Speech Therapist yet. That's part of the referral to the District Nurses. Andrea, you've organised that, haven't you?

Andrea: Not yet. I wanted to wait until after the team meeting. I'll ring this afternoon. So, can we put Lidia's expected date of discharge down as Friday, 9 June?

▬▬ 10.2

Nadine: District Nursing Service. Nadine Melesky speaking.

Andrea: Hello, it's Andrea here from 17 East at the Alexandra Hospital.

Nadine: I'm sorry. What was your name again, please?

Andrea: It's Andrea, Andrea Dubois from the Alexandra Hospital. I've got an 80-year-old lady I'd like to refer to you for some District Nursing services. Can I give you the details now?

Nadine: Wait a minute, let me get a referral form. OK, here it is. Yes, I'm ready, er, it was Andrea, wasn't it?

Andrea: That's right. Andrea Dubois from the Alexandra Hospital.

Nadine: Thanks, Andrea. Um, and what's the patient's name, please?

Andrea: I've got a Lidia Vassily for you.

Nadine: Oh, OK. Could you please spell that for me?

Andrea: Sure. It's L-I-D-I-A. She's Russian. And the surname's spelled V-A-double S-I-L-Y.

Nadine: Would you mind speaking a little slower, please? I'm having trouble following you.

Andrea: Yes, of course. It's hard over the phone, isn't it? Her family name is V-A-S-S-I-L-Y.

Nadine: Vassily, right. Double S, one L. Got it, thanks.

Andrea: Her address is 24 Spring Lane, Exeter. It's a bungalow. The spare key's with her daughter, Larissa. Her daughter's also her next of kin.

Nadine: OK. Do you have Lidia's home phone number, please?

Andrea: Yes, I've got it here. It's oh one two six five, six four four, seven five three.

Nadine: Could you please repeat that? I didn't catch the last numbers.

Andrea: Yes, sure. Where is it? Here we are: oh one two six five, six four four, seven five three. Did you get that?

Nadine: Yes, thanks. Oh one two six five, er, six four four, seven five three. Is that correct?

Andrea: Yes, that's right. Do you want me to give you her daughter's number, too?

Nadine: Yes, please.

Andrea: Her daughter's name is Larissa and she's Lidia's next of kin, as I said. Her phone number is oh one two six five, seven eight one, nine nine two.

Nadine: Oh one two six five, seven eight one, nine nine two. Thanks.

Andrea: Lidia's GP is Dr Serena Hanif. I'll spell that for you. It's H-A-N-I-F.

Nadine: Serena Hanif. Yes, OK. H-A-N-I-F.

Andrea: Lidia had a stroke three weeks ago. She's got moderate left-sided weakness and still has some difficulty swallowing. She needs quite a lot of help with her ADLs, especially bathing and mobility. She's quite unsteady on her feet and uses a walking frame.

Nadine: Does she have a walking frame or will I have to order one?

Andrea: No, it's OK. She's already got a walking frame. She might need a shower chair, though. I think it'd be better to wait until after she has a home assessment done before any aids are ordered. The home assessment has been booked for 12th June.

Nadine: Er, home assessment 12th June. That's Monday, 12th June, right?

Andrea: Yes, that's it. Lidia's daughter asked if you could let her know what time the home assessment's being done so she can come over to her mother's house. She and her sister are a great support. Lidia's house will need some adaptions and her daughters want some advice on the sort of aids which are available to make things easier.

Nadine: OK. How's she managed with her diet?

Andrea: She's been managing a soft diet for a few days now.

Nadine: Mm, soft diet. Does she need her meals delivered to her at home?

Andrea: No. Her daughters are very supportive, and they'll help her with shopping and meal preparation. They know the sort of food she likes. No, forty mg not fifty …

Nadine: Sorry, I didn't catch that.

Andrea: Oh, no, I'm sorry, Nadine, someone just asked me a question. I got distracted. Er, I think I've given you all the information you need. Her discharge summary will be sent to you in the next day or so. Is there anything else you need to know?

Nadine: No, I think I've got everything. Er, thanks for being patient with me.

Andrea: No problem and thanks for your help.

▬▬ 10.3

Simon: Good morning, 12 West, Simon speaking.

Gillian: Um, it's Gillian Bonham here. I'm Gilbert Bouchard's daughter. Am I speaking to one of the nurses?

Simon: Yes, it's Simon here. I'm a Staff Nurse on this ward.

Gillian: Right, um, I'm a little bit worried about my father, er, I don't want to be a nuisance, um …

Simon: Not at all. I'm happy to help you if I can. Actually, I'm the nurse who's looking after your father today.

Gillian: Oh, that's good. He's going home soon and everything's sorted out as far as that's concerned, but I've been worried about his moods lately. You never know how he's going to be, you know, if he's going to cry or laugh at the wrong time.

Simon: Mm, I can understand why you're concerned. It's quite hard for everyone to handle, isn't it?

Gillian: Oh, I'm glad you understand what I mean. It's quite embarrassing, um, I didn't want to say anything about it, but it's been quite difficult. He was never like this before. He always kept his emotions under control, but now he's like a different person.

Simon: Yes, I know what you mean. It can be quite difficult after a stroke. People who've had a stroke can be quite emotionally labile, you know. Their moods and emotions go up and down and sometimes their emotional responses don't match what they're really feeling. They might laugh even though they're very upset or cry when they're happy. I'll make a note in Mr Bouchard's notes and pass the message on to his Key Worker. She'll call you and talk to you about how you can help your father at home.

Gillian: That would be really helpful. I'm afraid I've felt like I don't know what's going on. It's so overwhelming.

Simon: I understand. Now, do we have your contact details on file?

Gillian: Yes. I gave the nurse my phone number yesterday. Er, have you got the results of the tests dad did yesterday?

Simon: I'm sorry, I'm afraid I can't talk to you about your father's results because of confidentiality. We can only discuss the results with you if your father gives us permission.

Gillian: Oh, yes. I forgot, the privacy laws.

Simon: That's right. But I can direct you to the Discharge Planning Nurse and you can discuss your concerns with him. His name's Stephen Wiseman. I'll give you his direct number in case I can't put you through.

Gillian: Thanks. I appreciate your help.

▬▬ 10.4

Katherine: Right, let's look at left CVA first. Ischaemia causes death of tissue on the left side of the brain. This causes damage to body functions on the right side of the body. In the case of a mild left CVA, it causes right hemiparesis, or right-sided weakness. More serious damage in a left CVA causes right hemiplegia, or right-sided paralysis.

Barbara: Of course, 'hemi' means half, doesn't it?

Katherine: That's right. Hemiparesis is weakness on one half of the body; hemiplegia is paralysis on one half of the body. Now your father had a left CVA which is affecting his right side. He's got right hemiparesis at the moment. You will have noticed that his body's quite weak on that side. The weakness affects the muscles around the mouth as well, and this is why swallowing's difficult. The damage caused is called dysphagia, or difficulty swallowing.

Barbara: I noticed that dad's eating puréed food.

Katherine: Yes, that's right. The other consequence of having weak muscles around the mouth is dysarthria, or difficulty articulating words. The muscles of the tongue and lips are also weak, so his speech is affected.

John: Dad's certainly having trouble with pronunciation; he just can't get the words out properly.

Katherine: Yes, the Speech and Language Therapist is also doing some exercises with him. The exercises help with dysarthria.

Barbara: Dad seems to have problems finding the right word, too. He often comes out with a word he doesn't mean to say. Why's that?

Katherine: That's because left CVA often causes speech and language problems. Some patients have aphasia, or an inability to communicate. Fortunately, your father is able to communicate, but he does have dysphasia, or difficulty expressing himself. That's why he says the wrong word for the thought he's trying to express.

John: It's a real problem, you know. It's really frustrating him. We don't know what to do. Sometimes he just starts crying.

Katherine: Mm, emotional lability is very common. It usually shows up as crying at inappropriate times, but it can also be laughing or giggling. Oh, it's very distressing, I know.

John: Oh, OK. Thanks for explaining that. We'll try to be more patient with him. He's also so slow at the moment. Why's that?

Katherine: You'll find that his behaviour pattern has changed. People who have had a left CVA tend to have a slow and cautious behaviour pattern. You'll need to repeat any instructions you give your father a few times before he'll understand them. That's also because he has memory loss: his short-term memory's been affected.

Barbara: Yes, we've noticed that. He can't remember something from five minutes ago but remembers our family holidays when John and I were children.

Katherine: Oh, and another important thing: there's absolutely no hearing loss during a stroke.

Barbara: Oh dear, I've been shouting a bit at dad thinking he couldn't hear properly. I'll stop doing that. He must've hated it.

Katherine: Don't worry, it's a common mistake.

10.5

Selena: The Pines care home.

Deanna: Hello, yes, it's Deanna Giles here from 4B at Alexandra Hospital. I have a patient transfer for you.

Selena: Oh, yes. I've been expecting a call from you. Can you fill me in about her, please?

Deanna: Sure. Her name is Ernesta Bortoli. That's Ernesta E-R-N-E-S-T-A and her surname is Bortoli. That's spelled B-O-R-T-O-L-I. She's an 87-year-old who had a left CVA six weeks ago. She's been here with us in Rehab for the past month and has been doing very well. Unfortunately, she just can't manage in her own home any more.

Selena: Well, we'll try to settle her in here. I'll have a lot of assessments to do on admission, but it's always useful to get an idea of how she's been managing her ADLs in Rehab.

Deanna: Sure. She's improved a lot over the last week. I've just done a Katz Index to assess her level of independence with ADLs. I'll go through it with you now if you like.

Selena: Thanks, it gives us a better idea of her needs. Just a minute. I'll just get one of our charts so I can fill it as you tell me. Right, I've got it. What did she score?

Deanna: Well, overall her score was two out of six, which puts her at moderate to high dependency.

Selena: OK, I'll just put that score at the bottom of the chart before we start.

Deanna: OK, bathing first. She scored a zero for bathing, as she needs assistance getting into the shower and can't manage to wash herself. You'll need to shower her on a shower chair with assistance. She has quite a lot of residual hemiparesis from the stroke.

Selena: Right, that would affect her ability to dress herself, too, wouldn't it? How does she manage?

Deanna: Not very well, I'm afraid. She scored a zero for dressing. She does have clothes which need minimal help – you know, Velcro wherever possible – but still needs the assistance.

Selena: What about toileting? What did she score for toileting?

Deanna: She isn't able to toilet herself either so that was a zero, too. She needs quite a lot of help getting on and off the toilet or commode.

Selena: And transferring?

Deanna: Actually she scored one for that. She uses a small frame to help with mobility and transfers quite well from bed to chair, for example. She also scored one for feeding. She's able to use modified utensils to eat. As she still eats a soft diet, she manages quite well.

Selena: So that just leaves continence.

Deanna: Ernesta is incontinent of urine. She uses pads during the day and night so she scores zero for continence.

Selena: Thanks for that information. We have a good programme here to encourage independence, so we'll try to work on those areas where Ernesta needs most help.

ANSWER KEY

Unit 1

1a
Suggested answers
1. The nurse is taking down patient details before the patient goes to the ward. Some admissions are done after the patient has arrived on the ward, in which case it is the ward staff who admit the patient.
2. The kind of information collected would be personal details such as name and contact number of next of kin, past medical and surgical history, and details of allergies.
3. Because it is important to alert staff to allergies and any problems in the patient's past medical or surgical histories.

b
1. Yes, with the help of a stick.
2. No, she hasn't.
3. She is being admitted to the Cardiac Unit.

c
2. Good morning, Shona.
3. How are you today?
4. Not too bad, thank you.
5. I'd like to ask you a few questions, if it's all right with you?
6. Yes, of course. That's fine.

d
1. She has high blood pressure and is in for some tests.
2. She had a mild heart attack.
3. No, she doesn't think she has any allergies.
4. Yes, her son, Jeremy Chad.

e
2 e   3 d   4 b   5 f   6 a
7 c

g
Suggested answers
1. You would assist the patient to sit down and make sure s/he was comfortable before starting with the admission. The patient's full name, including title, is used as a mark of respect. You may also use more formal language, for example *Would you mind if … , Could you … please.*
2. With children, the nurse would greet the child by his/her first name and use his/her own first name in return. The language used would be informal, for example *Can you … please.* You would put the child at ease and anticipate any anxiety about the hospital admission.
3. It is important to empathise with the patient and apologise for the wait. Reassure the patient that you will admit him/her as quickly as possible.

2a
Suggested answer
1. Active listening strategies are used to put the other person at ease, show interest in what is being said, and confirm understanding of what has been said. These include gestures, body position – for example, leaning towards the speaker – nodding, making 'listening noises', respecting personal space and maintaining comfortable eye contact.

b
1. *I see*
2. *mm/hm*
3. nodding your head
4. eye contact

c
Shona smiles, laughs, nods and leans towards Mrs Chad. She also uses *mm.*

3a
1. The cardiac cycle includes all events which occur from the beginning of one heartbeat to the beginning of the next heartbeat, for example systole and diastole.
2. The atria and ventricles contract and then the whole heart relaxes.
3. Shortness of breath, as not enough blood is oxygenated by the lungs.
4. The nurse in the Cardiac Unit is sometimes required to teach patients about the cardiac cycle in order to explain some of the cardiac tests or procedures which patients have before heart surgery.

b
the atria – receive blood
the ventricles – pump blood
the pulmonary artery – carries de-oxygenated blood to the lungs
the valves – open to allow blood to flow between the chambers and then close to prevent backflow of blood
the pulmonary vein – carries oxygenated blood from the lungs to the left atrium
the aorta – brings oxygenated blood to all parts of the body

4a
They are talking about lifestyle changes after a diagnosis of hypertension, which are needed to manage his blood pressure at home.

b
2 g   3 c   4 d   5 b   6 f
7 a

c
1. same level
2. positive
3. judgemental
4. rapport

1 d   2 a   3 b   4 c

d
Susanna sits at the same level as the patient, nods and uses humour to establish a rapport. She also uses *Mm, yeah.*

5a
Suggested answers
1. Handovers should alert nurses to the presence of IV therapy, drains, wounds, etc. Medication reviews and test results should be given. Staff should be informed of any tests or procedures which will occur during the next shift. Handovers should only give information about the changes in condition or treatment which have occurred during the relevant shift.

2. Patient details and treatment which are already noted on the printed handover sheet are not repeated – this is to save time, as the handover usually only lasts 20–30 minutes.
3. Inaccurate handing over of information can lead to medication errors, incorrect preparation for tests, and missing appointments with other healthcare professionals, for example X-ray.

b
1. Uncontrolled hypertension
2. She had a heart attack (myocardial infarction) in June.

c
1 T
2 T
3 F – BP 210/105
4 F – P was 100
5 T

d
2 m   3 b   4 f   5 l   6 c
7 j   8 h   9 e   10 n   11 d
12 a   13 k   14 i

e
2 MI
3 SHO
4 BP
5 ECG
6 GTN
7 O$_2$

f
2 10 pm
3 SHO
4 Oxygen
5 two hundred and twenty over one hundred
6 pulse
7 one twenty
8 five past ten
9 SHO
10 ECG
11 sublingual

6a
Suggested answers
3. Nursing and other healthcare professionals have access to these charts, which are often kept at the end of the patient's bed in an opaque plastic folder for privacy. However, the charts are easily accessed by the patient or friends and relatives of the patient.
4. The nurse who is looking after the patient is responsible for completing the chart. A student nurse may complete the chart if checked and countersigned by a qualified nurse.

b
1. She will be in hospital for three days.
2. Dr Fielding came to see her because her BP had increased and she was complaining of chest pain.
3. Jenny took her observations before giving the handover.

c

Time	P	BP
06.00	76	175/90
10.00	112	210/130
14.00	97	195/90
15.00	86	180/85

d
1 One hundred and ten over/on seventy
2 One hundred and fifty over/on ninety
3 One hundred and forty-two over/on ninety-nine
4 Eighty-six over/on forty

e
Suggested answers

↑	→	↓
shoot up to peak (maximum result)	settle remain the same to be constant to be steady	go down fall plummet (sudden decrease)

Unit 2

1a
1 The peak flow meter is used to measure how fast a person can blow out air after taking a big breath in.

b
1 Mrs Drake feels much better; her chest feels less tight and she is breathing more easily.
2 So that she can keep an eye on her asthma when she goes home.
3 At the same time each day.
4 To take the peak flow readings at the same time every day, write the result on her Daily Record Chart, and bring this to the Asthma Clinic.

c
1 Would you mind
2 I'd like you
3 could you

d
2 Now, stand up. Take a deep breath and try to fill your lungs as much as you can.
3 Next, blow as hard and as fast as you can with one breath.
4 Make a note of the final position of the marker.
5 After that, I want you to blow into the peak flow meter two more times.
6 The last thing to remember is to record the highest of the three readings on your Daily Record Chart.

f
In most of the instructions, the verb is an infinitive without to: blow, move, make, take. This is the most common and direct way of giving instructions and is appropriate after you have softened your request, for example: Would you mind … I'd like you to … Could you … . There are also useful phrases like I want you to … and The last thing to remember is … , both of which are followed by an infinitive with to.

2b
2 at the same level
3 That's right
4 I'm going to teach you how to …
5 understood
6 firstly, secondly; fingers
7 Demonstrate
8 Repeat

c
Eleanor states the purpose of the communication I'm going to show you how to use a peak flow meter today.
She smiles and nods at Mrs Drake.
She gives the instructions in steps I'll go through it with you step-by-step.
She encourages her Yes, you will! Don't worry, it'll become a habit.
She uses an appropriate level of language.
She demonstrates I'll just show you how to use the peak flow meter.
She gives her the opportunity to ask questions (Do you have any questions?).

3a
2 Bronchodilators (medication that makes the airway wider); inhalers and nebulisers to make breathing easier (a spacer is attached to make it easier for a child to use an inhaler); dust reduction in the home (vacuuming every day)

b
1 Put in the medication
2 Connect to the oxygen
3 Put on the mask
4 Turn on the oxygen
5 Breathe in the mist

c
1 c   2 e   3 a   4 d   5 b

d
Melanie states the purpose of the communication I'd just like to show you how to use this nebuliser.
She sits at the same level as Mr Dwyer so is non-threatening I'll bring a chair up so I can have a chat with you.
She smiles and nods at him; she gives the instructions in steps I'll go through all the steps with you.
She encourages Mr Dwyer It's not too difficult. I'm sure you'll catch on quickly.
She gives Mr Dwyer the opportunity to ask questions Any questions?

4a
2 oral cavity
3 voice box / larynx
4 bronchus
5 alveoli
7 epiglottis
8 windpipe / trachea
9 pleural membrane
10 intercostal space

b
1 The inner muscle of the asthmatic airway is inflamed so it is hard for air to go through.
2 An asthmatic makes a wheezing noise when trying to breathe during an asthma attack; they may also clutch their neck and look distressed.

c

	a		b	
1	a	H	b	A
2	a	A	b	H
3	a	H	b	A
4	a	A	b	H

d
1 becomes inflamed
2 is conducted
3 is exchanged
4 is narrowed
5 tighten
6 to breathe

The verbs in 1–4 are in the passive. The passive to be + past participle is often used to describe a process, for example … is conducted, … is exchanged, … is narrowed, … is produced. You can also use to become + past participle to describe a process, for example becomes swollen.

5b
2 level
3 simple
4 diagrams
5 decision-making
6 encouragement
7 appeal
8 cheerful
9 explain

c
Tim sits at the same level as Susie Can I come and sit here with you for a while?
He uses simple, clear sentences and checks for understanding Can you see that there is less room for air to go through?
He uses a diagram to illustrate his talk Have a look on the first page, and you'll see a diagram of what we call your respiratory system.
He involves Susie in decision-making Does that sound like a good idea?
He encourages Susie Good on you! I thought you'd find it interesting.
He uses a cheerful tone of voice.

6a
2 d   3 c   4 f   5 g   6 b
7 a

b
1 inspiration
2 inspiratory rate
3 respirations
4 respiratory rate
5 expiration
6 expiratory rate

d
1 Mr Frank's family are staying with him because he is dying.
2 Judy is managing the pain using a PCA with morphine.
3 The oxygen is being delivered by nasal cannulae (also called nasal prongs).
4 The tachypnoea was caused by a lung infection.

7a
1 Poorly managed asthma
2 Antibiotics
3 She is having a chest X-ray and the Respiratory Team is visiting.
4 Peak flow readings

b
2 f   3 a   4 c   5 b   6 d

d
1 Hourly
2 Three litres a minute
3 Because Mrs Castle became breathless.
4 30 minutes

e
RR at 06.00 was 18 breaths not 16
Pain score at 14.00 was 7/10 not 6/10
RR at 14.00 was 26 not 22
RTW on three litres of oxygen not four at 14.00
RR at 15.00 was 20 not 18

f
1 b   2 d   3 e   4 c   5 a

g
1 ap**noea**
2 brady**pnoea**
3 eu**pnoea**
4 tachy**pnoea**
5 dys**pnoea**

h
1 No, the *p* is not a silent letter in all words.
2 *Apnoea* and *eupnoea* don't have a silent *p*.

i
1 AE air entry; FBC full blood count
2 No, she is afebrile.
3 Fast, she has tachypnoea.
4 The day the report was written.
5 Yes, she has to start taking it again.

Unit 3

1a
Suggested answer
3 Possible complications with wound healing include infection, delayed healing, pain, lack of mobility and amputation.

b
1 She's removing the dressing on a leg wound
2 To make sure there is no cross-infection from the bacteria on her hands

c
1 For advice on the management of Mr Jones' wound
2 Venous ulcer
3 Two weeks

d
2 He developed a venous ulcer on his right ankle after he tripped on some stairs …
3 His local doctor had a look at it and asked the District Nurse to come and dress the wound at home.
4 Two weeks ago he was admitted to this ward to have an assessment of his circulation and to monitor his wound management.
5 He had a Doppler test done last week.
6 We sent a wound swab off, and we just got the results yesterday.
7 He's started on some IV antibiotics.

f
2 g   3 b   4 a   5 c   6 d
7 e

g
1 Because it was not healing at home.
2 A VAC dressing
3 To help the wound heal faster

2a
1 c   2 a   3 e   4 b   5 d

b
1 What do you think I should do with this ulcer?
2 What do you suggest we use? What would you recommend that we change to?
3 Would you mind giving me some advice on his wound care management?
4 What would you recommend that we change to? What do you suggest we use?
5 Do you think it's a good idea to try that instead of the dressing they're using now?

3a
1 **Suggested answers**
a Looks infected as it has pus in the wound. It looks red and sore.
b Looks black and uneven around the edges with yellowish material in the middle.
c Looks like it has dead tissue around the edges. It looks blackened and not healed.
d Looks red and dry.

b
2 a   3 b   4 g   5 d   6 e
7 f   8 c

c
1 necrosis
2 es**char**
3 desic**cation**
4 inflam**mation**
7 debride**ment**
8 cellulitis

e
1 eschar (photo c)
2 cellulitis; desiccation (photo d)
3 inflammation; swab (photo a)
4 slough; debridement (photo b)

Share your knowledge
Suggested answers
1 The location of the ulcers would make it difficult to apply a wound dressing and mobilisation would be a problem.
2 Diabetics should never go barefoot as nerve damage decreases awareness of sensations in the foot and so injury in the form of skin cracks often goes unnoticed. These can lead to ulcers.
3 A consequence of diabetic ulcers can be a non-healing wound and ultimately amputation of the foot.

4b
high bacterial load, necrotic tissue, exudate

c
2 g   3 h   4 e   5 f   6 b
7 d   8 a

e
2 base
3 inflammation
4 balance
5 necrosis
6 load
7 exudate
8 dryness

f
2 Debridement
3 surgical
4 well-vascularised
5 infection
6 antibiotic
7 Reduced
8 imbalance
9 Excessive
10 Desiccation
11 dressings

12 fluid
13 optimal
14 chronic
15 Reassess
16 graft
17 advanced

5a
2 An estimated 15–20% of dog bite wounds become infected. Although rare, if infections aren't treated they may lead to septic arthritis or generalised sepsis. Dog bites in areas where rabies is present is also a problem.
3 Complications can be avoided by seeking medical treatment as soon as possible and keeping up-to-date with tetanus protection.

b
1 Puncture wounds
2 Flushed with normal saline, not sutured, dressed daily

c
1 c   2 a   3 d   4 b

d
2 He was treated in A&E and discharged home.
3 The wound became infected and he has returned to hospital.
4 The wound was reassessed yesterday.
5 Gary was started on IV antibiotics to clear up the infection in the wound.
6 The wound was surgically debrided this morning.
7 Gary returned to the ward with an antimicrobial dressing which will be re-dressed tomorrow.
8 He is in for a review by the Vascular Team on Monday.

e
2 d   3 i   4 k   5 a   6 j
7 f   8 l   9 c   10 h   11 b
12 e

f
1 **gran**ulated
2 **slough**y
3 **macer**ated
4 **inflam**ed
5 **ser**ous
6 haemo**ser**ous
7 **pur**ulent
8 **od**our
10 anti**micro**bial
11 **hydr**ating
12 **intact** wound

i
1 N/A
2 tds
3 bd
4 L
5 IV
6 amt

j
L calf, sloughy, infected, daily, IV, inflamed, small amt, purulent, yes (odor present), surgical, antimicrobial, open wound, for review by Vascular Team on Mon, wound intact – next dressing in two days

Unit 4

1a
3 The nurse may be discussing aspects of the patient's care with her.

b

1 To have a Personal Care Plan set up
2 Her local doctor
3 She couldn't control her blood sugar level at home.

c

1 F – the hospital referred her
2 F – she doesn't have one yet
3 T

d

1 How often
2 How many times
3 How frequently
4 Do you ever
5 Do you always

2a

Oh dear, that's a shame; Mm. Yes … ; Mm, I see; That's good; Oh, that's a pity; Mm; Oh, that's not so good

3a

1 Lifestyle changes include stopping smoking, exercising more, losing weight, eating a healthy diet and cutting down alcohol intake.

c

2 need to
3 Try to
4 should
5 good idea
6 must
7 important to
8 might like to

e

2 a   3 d   4 c   5 b   6 f
7 e

4a

1 To produce digestive enzymes and secrete them into the small intestine via the pancreatic duct.
2 To release hormones into the bloodstream; the beta cells of the islet cells in the pancreas secrete the hormone insulin into the bloodstream.
3 It lowers them.
4 Glucagon

5a

2 e   3 d   4 j   5 b   6 h
7 f   8 a   9 g   10 i

b

1 **pan**creas
2 diabe**tes**
3 diabe**tic**
4 hypogly**cae**mia
5 hypogly**cae**mic agent
6 gluco**suria**
7 **ke**tones
8 diabetic ketoaci**dosis**
9 **in**sulin
10 **blood** sugar level

c

2 regulates
3 glucose
4 fat/liver
5 liver/fat
6 fuel
7 beta
8 normalise
9 children
10 injections

11 90%
12 oral
13 inhalers/pumps
14 pumps/inhalers

e

Option 1: c
Option 2: a
Option 3: b

f

2 catheter
3 bolus
4 large swings
5 vial
6 disposable
7 Varying
8 mixed
9 accurate doses
10 convenient
11 cartridge
12 Pre-filled
13 convenient
14 end

6a

1 Times of BSL testing and results, times and results of urinalysis, and times of hypos
2 Five times a day
3 Her urine (tested for glucose and ketones)
4 She is given lemonade.
5 She checks her BSL again.

b

1 T
2 F – she is 85
3 T
4 T
5 T
6 F – should be less than 10 mmols 1½ hours after meals
7 T
8 F – it went up to 15
9 T
10 T

c

Hypo at 09.00, not 03.00; BSL 4.1 after lemonade; 7.1 at 16.30 yesterday; 8.0 at 02.00 today; 5.2 at 11.30 today; 4.8 at 21.30 today; no hypo today.

d

Suggested answer
Her diabetes is poorly managed.

▬▬ Unit 5

1a

Suggested answers
1 Blood, urine and other specimens are checked for things like electrolyte levels, presence of infective agents, sensitivity to antibiotics and presence of diagnostic agents for particular diseases, for example specific enzymes.
2 To monitor the progress of their patients, to check for toxicity of a drug before administration, to monitor infection and decide on changing patient precaution code (standard precaution to special precaution).

b

1 It hurts when she passes urine and she needs to pass urine frequently.
2 UTI
3 Culture and Sensitivity test (C&S)
4 A midstream urine specimen (MSU)

2b

1 c   2 b   3 d   4 e   5 a

c

1 Repeat
2 Paraphrase
3 intonation
4 clarify

3a

2 You need to clean the area around the urethra from front to back with these disposable wipes.
3 Don't touch inside the container when you take the lid off.
4 Try to catch the middle part of the urine stream.
5 Tighten the lid before you give me the specimen container, please.

b

1 a   2 c   3 b   4 d

4a

Suggested answers
2 Features of a good communication system include: records time of paging, easy to use, alerts staff member when page has been received.
3 Mobile phones are often used in place of pagers and email is also used. Technology is also changing the way nurses document patient information; for example, care plans are computerised rather than hand-written, cutting down time and limiting errors caused by illegible handwriting. Some hospital pharmacies use a bedside computerised system to order and supply patient medication, reducing the amount of time spent visiting hospital pharmacies to pick up scripts.

b

1 F – she is calling to tell the doctor the patient has frequency and burning when she passes urine
2 T
3 F – the doctor will come and write up some antibiotics in fifteen minutes
4 T

c

2 remind me
3 in for
4 complaining of
5 febrile
6 up a bit
7 malaise
8 MSU
9 write up
10 Pathology Form

5b

1 To filter the blood and remove waste products, which are secreted in urine
2 Nephrons
3 The renal medulla
4 The bladder
5 The urethra

6a

2 i   3 g   4 b   5 h   6 a
7 d   8 f   9 c   10 k   11 j
12 m   13 l

b
1 urinalysis
2 urine
3 urinal
5 renal
7 proteinuria
8 haematuria
9 specimen
10 oedema
11 anuria
12 nephrons
13 oliguria

d
1 T
2 F – it's the first stage.
3 T
4 F – it requires dialysis or transplant.
5 F – in early stages there are often no symptoms.

e
2 nephrons
3 toxic
4 renal failure
5 urine
6 oedema
7 lethargic
8 renal transplant

7a
1 An ordinary sample
2 Proteinuria, haematuria, pH value

b
The words *just* and *only* are missing.
1 I'd **just** like you to do it now, if that's all right.
2 I **just** need an ordinary sample of urine.
3 It **only** takes a few minutes to get a reading.
4 I'm checking for proteinuria; that **just** means protein in the urine.
5 **Just** ring when you want me to collect it.

d
The use of *just* and *only* softens the tone of the sentences.

8a
Suggested answers
2 Patients who are immobile because of surgery, suffering from a spinal cord injury, etc.
3 Infection and tissue damage
4 New developments in self-catheterisation include catheters with a low-friction outer coating. They are disposable, so more expensive, but carry fewer infections risks.

b
1 Not being able to pass urine (urinary retention)
2 Insert an indwelling catheter
3 A drainage bag

c
1 pass urine
2 in situ
3 contamination
4 transparent

d
2 f   3 a   4 c   5 b   6 e

9a
Suggested answers
2 Pathology Reports contain information about the analysis of specimens, presence of infective agents, cells which are visible under microscopy, and the sensitivity of the organisms to various antibiotics.
3 They are consulted before giving medications; to check on results of specimens which have been tested; and to check blood results, for example for anaemia.
5 The nurse will phone the doctor if an abnormal result comes in, particularly if it is serious.

b
1 Urine microbiology
2 Microscopy
3 MSU
4 18.45 on 6 March
5 07.18 on 7 March
6 Increased leucocytes, increased erythrocytes and the presence of bacteria
7 A bacterium
8 Antibiotics
9 That it showed a possible UTI

c
2 sensitive
3 bacteria
4 Microbes
5 antimicrobial
6 microbiology
7 erythrocytes
8 pathology
9 Microscopy
10 culture

Share your knowledge
Suggested answers
1 To determine whether it is viral (not treatable with antibiotics), bacterial (treatable with antibiotics) or fungal (treatable with anti-fungals). Also to identify the appropriate antibiotic which the infection is sensitive to.
2 More and more people are becoming resistant to antibiotics, so larger doses of antibiotics are needed to fight the infection if it recurs.
3 Methicillin Resistant Staphylococcus Aureus, also called *golden staph*, may cause cellulitis, wound infections and other serious infections.
4 It is a serious problem in almost all hospitals in the world.

▓▓ Unit 6

1a
Suggested answer
4 Controlled drugs are regulated so strictly because they are highly addictive and illegal without a prescription. They must be controlled to avoid street use.

b
1 She needs another nurse to check the morphine because it is a controlled drug.
2 An injection of morphine
3 He has to prepare a patient for the Operating Theatre.
4 Yes. She is clearing the dressing trolley, and then she is free.

c
1 c   2 a/d   3 a/d   4 b

d
Have you got a minute? – b
Are you free at the moment? – a
Are you busy at the moment or can you do a drug check with me? – d
Would you mind checking this morphine with me, please? – c

e
1 eyeballs
2 snowed
3 flat out
4 run off

All of the expressions mean *very busy.*

2a
1 Pethidine 100mg IM
2 Because Anna is carrying the CD keys so she can unlock the drug cupboard
3 Count how many ampoules are in the cupboard and confirm the number left when one is removed
4 They both have to sign the drug book.
5 The dose (100mg) and the expiry date (April, 2010)

b
2 Check the time the last injection was given to the patient
3 Get an ampoule from the locked cupboard
4 Check the number of ampoules left in the cupboard
5 Sign and witness the drug book
6 Check the expiry date of the drug in the ampoule
7 Draw up the correct amount of the drug in a syringe
8 Check the amount of drug drawn up in the syringe

d
2 f   3 d   4 a   5 c   6 e

3
2 f   3 a   4 b   5 e   6 d

Share your knowledge
Suggested answers
1 Team nursing is a type of nursing model which makes use of the different skill levels of the team and allows for the different scopes of practice between RNs and other levels of nursing, for example Assistant Nurses, Enrolled Nurses and Healthcare Assistants (HCAs). Team nursing was introduced in the 1950s to cope with post-war staff shortages. It regained popularity in the 1990s as a way of dealing with staff shortages.
2 Working as a team, each member encouraged to make suggestions, can lead to fewer staff absences as there is a shared workload.
3 Often viewed as *task allocation nursing*, where a task – for example, taking all observations – is allocated to one nurse; this can lead to boredom, potential problems with accountability, and become divisive, with some nurses taking on the heavier workload while others write the Patient Record.

4a
Answers

1 Medications which regulate the heartbeat; anticoagulant medication such as warfarin; insulin; and IV antibiotics. These may have serious side effects which may occur rapidly, for example increased bleeding or a drop in blood sugar level.
2 To check on the blood level of the drug, especially if the dose is adjusted accordingly.

b

1 He wants her to check a medication (warfarin) with him.
2 Chris Multer in bed 1
3 An anticoagulant medication
4 The INR
5 Josh signs and Susanna countersigns

c

2 Crosscheck chart and patient information
3 Check the medication label
4 Crosscheck route
5 Crosscheck time of administration
6 Check the INR result
7 Crosscheck dose on Medication Chart
8 Take out medication
9 Sign Medication Chart
10 Countersign Medication Chart

Share your knowledge
Suggested answer

3 Some units have introduced dedicated Medication Nurses who are responsible for handing out all medications. The pros are that they get less distracted by other tasks, can concentrate better, have less time pressure and are not interrupted while completing their round. The cons are that some nurses feel uncomfortable having another nurse dispense medication to 'their' patients, as they feel they aren't accountable for total patient care.

5a
Suggested answers

1 Because nurses are well placed to spend time answering questions and addressing patient concerns.
2 An incorrect dose may be taken, the wrong drug may be taken, and precautions may not be followed.
3 Interactions, special precautions, contraindications, and storage of the drug.

b

1 F – it lowers cholesterol levels
2 T
3 F – it's absorbed in the stomach and small intestine
4 T
5 F – it's better to take it in the morning

c

2 passes into
3 leads to
4 mixes with
5 goes into
6 via
7 metabolised
8 causes
9 inhibiting
10 released into

6a

1 Those which decrease the elimination of the drug from the body, for example erythromycin and cyclosporine. Warfarin and niacin are also contraindicated.
2 The build-up of the drug could cause muscle damage.
3 Grapefruit juice and related fruit such as Seville oranges

b

1 advised not to
2 should/must not be taken; increasing the risk
3 should be
4 must not take
5 should/must not be taken; increases the toxic effects
6 precaution to take

c

1 Her weekly rounds in the ward
2 Mr Albiston's chart
3 She noticed that Mr Albiston had been ordered a multi B vitamin, which is contraindicated with atorvastatin.
4 Vitamin B3
5 Helen will notify the doctor to cancel the order.

d

1 need to be
2 I'm a bit concerned
3 shouldn't be
4 shouldn't take
5 not to

7a
Suggested answers

1 It is a Prescription Chart.
3 It shows the name of the medication, the dose, the number of times the medication is to be given, the prescribing doctor's details and the date of the drug order.
4 The pharmacist, the doctor and the nurse are responsible for the chart.
5 It is updated each time a new medication is ordered or when a drug must be reordered.

b

2 f	3 d	4 g	5 e	6 i
7 a	8 c	9 j	10 b	

c

po; mg; mane

e

1 27 April
2 08.00
3 Yes, he has had three doses
4 A multi B vitamin
5 No
6 You would not give Mr Albiston a multi B vitamin at the same time as atorvastatin because of the drug interaction.

8b

1 The right drug
2 The right patient
3 The right route
4 The right dose
5 The right time

c

1 c   2 e   3 d   4 a   5 b

Unit 7

1a

2 When dehydrated, after surgery, to administer IV medications

b

1 An IV pump, a new bag of IV fluid hanging up ready to be started and a small bag of fluid going through an IV line which is also ready to be connected.
2 Reviewing IV fluids, discussing fluid intake and output

c

1 T
2 F – Paula is looking after Mrs Boland while Mrs Boland's nurse is off the ward
3 F – they are quite low
4 F – she is to start 1L Normal Saline with KCl 40 millimols
5 T
6 F – the cannula is going to be removed

d

2 a   3 a   4 a   5 a   6 b
7 a

e

1 Could you take down Mrs Boland's IV when it's finished, please?
2 Leave it (the cannula) for another day ...
3 Could you start her on a litre of Normal Saline with 40 millimols of KCl?
4 Can you run it over eight hours, please?
5 Can you take out his cannula before he goes home, please?

2a

C – Light dressing ✓
B – Take down IV when thr.
D – Run IV 8°
D – IV ABs
B – Leave cannula
D – K levels
C – Home this pm
D – Put up 1L N/S with KCl 40 mmols
C – Cannula out ✓

b

Because these tasks have already been done.

c

2 He said to leave the IV cannula in for another day just in case she needs more fluids.
3 He asked if you could put up a bag of Normal Saline with 40 mmols of KCl.
4 He wants it to run over eight hours.
5 He said that Mr Claussen's IV cannula could be taken out.

Share your knowledge
Suggested answers

4 Advantages of preloaded IV infusions: decreased bacterial contamination, accurate dose of additive is ensured, less chance of medication error, more convenient, decreased nurse time in preparing IV solutions with additives. Disadvantages: cost, possibility of mistaking dose (IV bags are loaded with 22 mmols KCl, 30 mmols KCl or 40 mmols KCl, with no colour coding to alert of different dose)

3a

1 To see that the IV cannula is in order before she puts up another infusion
2 Warmth, redness, tenderness
3 Six
4 It was in an inconvenient spot, which made the IV positional – that is, the IV stopped dripping when Mrs Boxmeer moved her arm.
5 The IV cannula is removed.

b

2 f   3 i   4 e   5 g   6 b
7 h   8 d   9 a

c

1 nosocomial
2 phlebitis
3 infiltration
4 Staph
5 IV giving set
6 erythema
7 aseptic technique
8 positional

e

2 put; in
3 put in
4 take out
5 leave; out
6 put in
7 put; in
8 put; in
9 take; out
10 take; out
11 kept in

4a

Suggested answers

1 Nurses would use the telephone to report test results, report a change in a patient's condition, request SHO to review a patient, request medication order, book tests, book porters, etc.
2 Nurses might receive the following types of information by phone: information relating to patient care, e.g. test results; phone orders for medication (in some countries); messages for patients from family or friends.
4 You can avoid misunderstandings when taking phone messages by asking the caller to repeat any information which you have not understood immediately, asking the caller to speak slowly if you can't understand, always noting down the message and asking about words you don't understand, and always asking for unusual words or names to be spelt out.

b

Dr Gonzalez; resite cannula Mrs Szubansky; Michael to call re when cannula needs resite; due time of next ABs; bleep Dr G on 645

c

2 Sorry, I didn't catch the patient's name. Could you spell it for me, please?
3 ... so you need to talk to Mrs Szubansky's nurse about resiting a cannula?
4 Would you mind slowing down a bit? I'm afraid I've missed some of the message.
5 OK. Let me just read that message back to you.
6 I'll make sure I pass on your message to Michael. He's the nurse looking after Mrs Szubansky today.
7 Can I get a contact number so Michael can return your call?

Share your knowledge

Suggested answers

1 Other ways messages can be passed on include writing the message on the ward whiteboard or message board, or sending an SMS if nurses use mobile phones to send and receive messages.
3 Some problems that occur when messages have to be passed on include the ward or unit not having a prominent place to display messages so the messages are not noted, staff taking messages without making a written note and then forgetting to pass them on, messages not being understood correctly and not being passed on because of embarrassment, and messages not being passed on in a timely manner and being forgotten.

5a

1 The chart is used to order IV infusions.

b

1 She's going on a break.
2 Because she was receiving IV antibiotics when she was first admitted
3 Normal Saline
4 To check out the next IV infusion as the current infusion has just finished
5 Miss Hadfield's details, the time the current litre started, the time it finished, the amount of fluid that went through, the next order (date, route (IVI), name of solution)
6 The name of the solution and the expiry date
7 The infusion rate
8 Both nurses
9 The expiry date

c

2 8
3 03.00
4 11.00
5 1000 ml
6 30th
7 5%
8 30th
9 5%
10 16th
11 2010
12 11.00
13 10
14 1000 ml
15 100 ml

6a

2 It records fluid intake and output in order to assess fluid status.
3 It is the responsibility of each nurse to fill out the chart for his/her shift.

b

2 UTT
3 BO
4 C/F
5 U/O
6 H_2O
7 BNO
8 Sml amt
9 Wet bed +
10 OJ
11 to KVO
12 Asp
13 Mod amt

c

1 Miss Stavel's Fluid Balance Chart
2 It isn't accurate.
3 Her daily weight
4 No intake record 10 am–5 pm
04.00 Wet bed+
05.00 Vomit Lge amt
08.00 Wet bed++
Hasn't passed urine since lunchtime
13.00 (U/O) UTT
17.00 Amount ½ cup; Vomit Sml amt

d

2 recorded; inaccurately
3 measure; properly
4 problem; record
5 accuracy
6 point; mistakes

e

1 It's impossible to know what size cup!
2 It really doesn't look as though it was explained to her at all.
3 ... they haven't been able to measure it properly.

▆ Unit 8

1a

Suggested answers

2 Pre-op checking procedures ensure that all information is correct, for example: correct identity of the patient, consent form signed, correct preparation made for the operation, etc.
3 Incorrect checking could lead to the wrong patient being taken to the Operating Theatre, the wrong pre-med being given, Theatre staff not being alerted to allergies, and a patient who has not fasted pre-operatively vomiting during surgery.

b

1 Mrs Clarke has to wash twice with antiseptic wash – once the evening before the operation and once on the morning of the operation. She also has to remove her nail polish.
2 Because it's a choking risk with anaesthesia
3 To prevent DVTs

c

2 I'll
3 you'll
4 Will
5 I'm going to
6 won't; will
7 I'll; You'll

2a

Suggested answers

2 When dealing with children and non-native speakers of English, it is a good idea to show them any pieces of equipment or show pictures of what to expect after an operation.
3 Pre-op patient education has been shown to improve patient compliance with any post-op activities, for example post-op exercises. It also decreases patient anxiety and lessens the experience of pain. Benefits to the healthcare system include reduced days in hospital and less likelihood of return to hospital with avoidable complications.

b

1 d   2 e   3 b   4 c   5 a

3a

1 Before surgery it is important to explain about IVs, IDCs, drains and dressings which the patient will return with. Post-operative activities – for example, deep breathing and coughing – may need to be explained. Preventative measures such as anti-embolic stockings and heparin injections should also be explained.

3 The challenges include the rapid pace, pre-op and post-op care being demanding, pain management, and the quick turnover of patients.

4 Laparoscopic, or keyhole, surgery has become more widespread.

5 Patients are prepared for abdominal surgery by having a low residue diet for a few days and then a clear fluid diet coupled with an enema to ensure the bowel is clear. The abdominal area may be shaved according to the surgeon's wishes.

b

2 d   3 a   4 c   5 f   6 b

d

1 Very anxious
2 Keyhole surgery, also called minimally invasive surgery
3 A laparoscope
4 The surgery is performed through three to four small puncture sites instead of a long incision.
5 A couple of hours
6 Emma's swallow reflex
7 Soon after returning to the ward, when Emma thinks she can pass urine.

e

2 f   3 h   4 d   5 a   6 c
7 g   8 b

4a

Suggested answers

1 Spend time explaining what happens in the pre-op and post-op period so it is more familiar. Ensure that you have uninterrupted time to discuss any concerns with your patient so that they feel comfortable talking about them. Be aware of cultural or language factors which may cause more anxiety and ensure an interpreter is at hand if necessary.

2 Yes, different strategies may be needed depending on the needs of the particular age group.

3 Strategies useful for a child: allow the child to touch equipment, for example oxygen masks; reassure the child that a parent will accompany them to the Operating Theatre; allow the child to take a special toy with them or keep the toy to wait for the child.

4 Strategies for a patient who doesn't speak English: ensure that an interpreter is available to translate your instructions and the patient's questions; be culturally sensitive to any concerns the patient may have; allow the interpreter or relative to accompany the patient to Operating Theatres.

b

2 reassuring
3 normal
4 anxiety
5 avoid
6 involve

c

1 That she might overdose
2 Alva explains the 'lock-out' feature, which prevents patients over-using the PCA.
3 The nurses will check her obs. and her pain level second hourly (required during the use of a PCA).
4 Emma will use her tri-ball every hour whilst she is awake.
5 That she must wear TEDs until fully mobile.

d

1 c   2 d   3 a   4 e   5 b

5a

It shows a patient with DVT.

b

1 T
2 F – he had the symptoms after this operation
3 T
4 F – only on the affected leg
5 F – he hasn't developed a pulmonary embolism
6 F – he has warmth, swelling and calf pain

c

1 c   2 d   3 a   4 b

d

1 venodilation
2 embolus
3 embolism
4 venous stasis

e

1 normal blood flow
2 DVT
3 embolus
4 embolism

f

1 Venous stasis caused by immobility
2 Venodilation causes small tears in the inner walls of the veins
3 Blood becomes stickier and coagulates more easily
4 Formation of an embolus
5 An embolus blocks blood flow

g

2 heparin
3 subcutaneous
4 warfarin
5 DVTs; pulmonary embolism; lifelong
6 dose; INR
7 filter

6a

1 The chart is used to check a patient before going to an operation.

b

1 YES   2 YES   3 YES   4 YES
5 NO   6 NO   7 NO   8 NO
9 NO   10 YES   11 YES   12 N/A
13 YES 14 YES
Fluid last given at 11 pm
Urine last voided at 10.20 am
Food last given at 6 pm
Catheterised N/A

c

Name
ID bracelet
Operation or procedure
Consent form signed
Pre-med given and signed for

d

2 I'm just going to go through this Checklist again.
3 I know you've already answered many of these questions, but we like to double-check everything.
4 Can you tell me your full name, please?
5 I'll have a quick look at your identification bracelets if I may?
6 Can you tell me what operation you're having today?
7 Did you sign a consent form for the operation?
8 Is this your signature on the consent form?
9 Have you had a pre-med?
10 I'll sign the Checklist, and you've already got a theatre cap to cover your hair.

Share your knowledge
Suggested answer

3 Having several checks before the patient has an operation guards against: mistaken identity; the wrong operation being performed; lack of consent leading to a charge of negligence and/or assault and battery; potentially serious allergies being missed.

Unit 9

1a
Suggested answers

2 Name of operation performed, any complications, analgesia given in Recovery, any complications in Recovery, drains and dressings in situ, new Prescription Charts (IV Infusion Orders), medication orders and follow-up instructions. All pre-op charts also need to be handed back, with new orders on new charts, and the Operation Report.

3 The Ward Nurse crosschecks the Operation Report, Prescription Chart, Obs. Chart, the patient's wound, drains and IV.

4 All previous orders (Prescription Charts, medication and dressings) have changed.

5 It's important to check for excessive blood loss, pain level, dehydration, nausea and vomiting, and loss of consciousness.

b

1 He's had a splenectomy.
2 Because he was slow to wake up after his operation.
3 Because he had some post-op nausea and vomiting.
4 Yes, it is patent and draining.
5 Using clips
6 No, it is to be left intact for the surgeon to review the next day.
7 Yes, in Recovery
8 He was feeling cold and his temperature was a bit low.

c

2 a   3 e   4 c   5 b   6 d

d

2 13/15
3 36°
4 72
5 97
6 dextrose
7 patent
8 Clips
9 NAD
10 75
11 oral
12 redivac
13 intact

2a
1 No, he's still a bit hypothermic.
2 Some ice chips
3 No, he feels sick.
4 No, he's in a lot of pain.
5 No, because he has a urinary catheter in situ.
6 He can use the call bell to call the nurse.

b
2 e   3 h   4 g   5 b   6 d
7 f   8 a

3a
1 Six at rest, seven on movement
2 It reduces the amount of opioids needed.
3 She gives him some analgesia, puts him in a comfortable position, pulls the curtains and dims the lights.

b
1 hurt
2 throbbing
3 hurts
4 stinging
5 knife

c
2 a   3 f   4 b   5 g   6 h
7 d   8 e

Share your knowledge
Suggested answers
1 Pain can be described as aching, cramping, crushing, throbbing, radiating.
2 For example: an aching knee, cramping period pain, crushing angina pain, throbbing headache, radiating heart attack pain
3 Pain behaviours include intermittent moaning, rubbing the affected area, grimacing, limping, constantly changing position
4 These behaviours draw attention to their pain.
5 Possible pain management problems include: sufferers feel that they are not taken seriously and can become quite hostile, sufferers may not want to try new options for fear of an increase in pain, constant moaning can make empathetic response a challenge.

4b
1 They are watching a patient and his visitors, as the visitors appear to be becoming agitated.
2 He is upset that Paul is in pain and thinks the nurses are not helping him.
3 They speak calmly and offer to get Paul some pain relief.
4 She asks him to lower his voice.
5 She reassures him that Paul is getting regular pain relief and says she will talk to Paul about alerting the nursing staff earlier if the amount of pain medication is not enough.

c
2 defuse
3 Listen
4 Speak
5 Rephrase
6 Empathise
7 solution
8 alternative

d
Listen calmly – use non-verbal communication such as nodding the head, maintaining comfortable eye contact and making 'listening noises' to reinforce that you are interested in what the speaker is saying.
Defuse the situation if possible – *It's OK, I'll see what I can do. I'll be looking after Paul this evening. Can I ask who you are first, please?*
Speak quietly but firmly – *I need you to lower your voice so we can talk about sorting out Paul's pain.*
Rephrase – *You're worried that Paul isn't getting regular pain relief. Is that right?*
Empathise – *I do understand, its hard, isn't it?*
Offer a solution – *How about I get his chart now and see what he's been having?*

Share your knowledge
Suggested answers
1 Aggressive behaviour is a problem in many countries. Statistically, nurses are more likely to be attacked than any other healthcare workers.
2 The reasons for aggression can be frustration with treatment, dissatisfaction with staffing levels, past history of aggression or having a short fuse, parents with children in pain, drug and alcohol withdrawal, feelings of loss of autonomy especially when used to being in control of situations, fear of pain, dementia, different images of nurses in different cultures.
3 Initiatives include having a good ABM programme in each hospital, good support for nurses' safety from management, signs alerting patients that aggression towards nursing staff will not be tolerated, cultural awareness training regarding differing images of nurses.

5a
1 An injury to the skin, for example a surgical incision
2 Visceral pain
3 Type A-delta and Type C
4 Fast pain is acute and localised; slow pain is aching and referred.
5 Pain relief

b
2 a   3 d   4 b   5 f   6 c

c
1 **no**ciceptor
2 **cuta**neous
3 **vis**ceral
4 **incis**ion
5 **loca**lised pain
6 referred pain

d
2 c   3 h   4 g   5 d   6 b
7 i   8 e   9 a

e
2 threshold
3 tolerance
4 scale
5 non-steroidal
6 morphine-like
7 background
8 Multimodal

Share your knowledge
Suggested answer
1 If pain isn't adequately treated it can affect a patient's ability to mobilise after surgery or to do important post-op exercises. Chronic pain can lead to depression.

6a
1 The chart is for rating pain intensity and contains a number of different scales.
3 The facial expressions, often called The Wong–Baker faces, are used to rate the level of pain felt by a child or a person who is unable to communicate verbally because of a language barrier or other problem.
4 The numerical scale, which uses numbers from 0 (no pain) to 10 (worst pain imagined by the sufferer); the verbal descriptor; and the activity tolerance scale.
5 Pain levels are subjective so it is important that the patient be able to describe their pain.

b
1 Stickers
2 Number three
3 A video game

c
2 f   3 a   4 b   5 e   6 c

d
1 don't you?
2 isn't he?
3 is he?
4 doesn't it?
5 shall we?
Sharon uses question tags to soften what she says and to include Anton in the conversation.

f
b 5   c 3   d 4   e 1   f 6
g 7

Share your knowledge
1 Other groups who can use the Wong–Baker faces scale include anyone who has difficulty verbalising, due to lack of language skills or as the result of an illness such as dysphasia.
2 The chart could be modified by using Braille so that visually impaired patients could feel the faces.
3 The faces could be modified to show examples of emotions; for example, anger, fear, grief or incomprehension.

▇▇▇ Unit 10

1a
Suggested answers
1 To avoid duplication of services, to ensure a holistic approach to patient care
2 Communication problems, poor sense of teamwork

b
1 T
2 F – they found her uncoordinated
3 F – she'd had a stroke
4 F – it happened the night before
5 T
6 F – it is planned
7 T

c
1 Two weeks
2 To go back to her own home
3 Monday, 12 June
4 The kitchen staff puréed food brought in for her
5 With her daughter, Larissa
6 Friday, 9 June

d
2 a   3 b   4 c   5 c   6 b